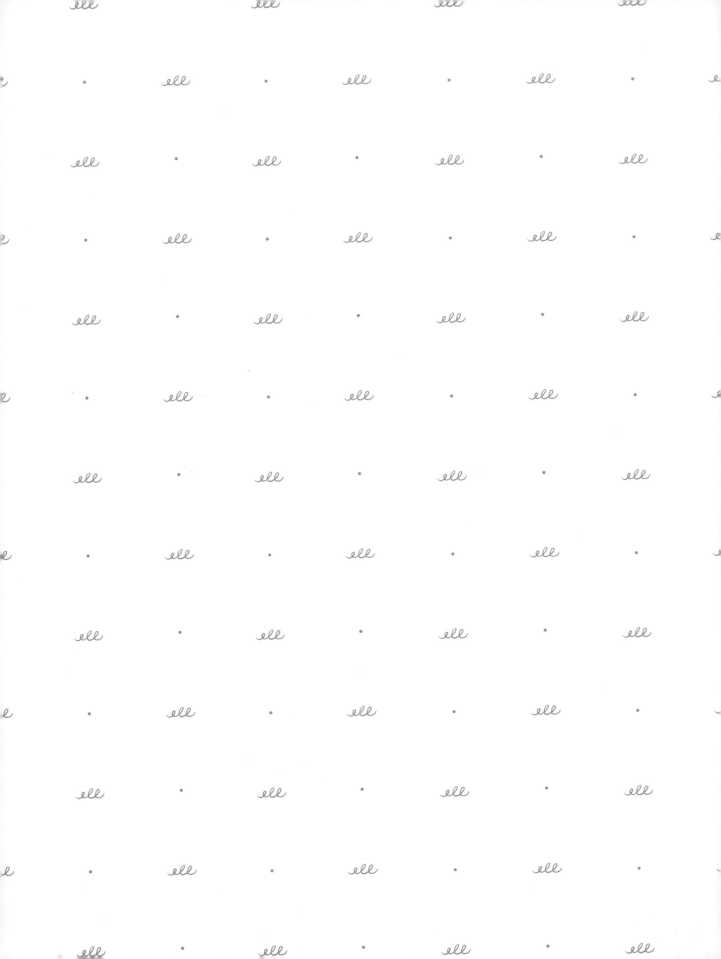

The Simplified Cookbook

delicious meals with effortless prep

EMILY LEY

THOMAS NELSON

Since 1798

Published in Nashville, Tennessee, by Thomas Nelson. Thomas Nelson is a registered
trademark of HarperCollins Christian Publishing, Inc.

Photography by Kris D'Amico, Whitney Hawkins, and Carly Tanner.

Thomas Nelson titles may be purchased in bulk for educational, business, fund-raising, or sales
promotional use. For information, please email SpecialMarkets@ThomasNelson.com.

Any internet addresses, phone numbers, or company or product information printed in this book are offered
as a resource and are not intended in any way to be or to imply an endorsement by Thomas Nelson, nor does
Thomas Nelson vouch for the existence, content, or services of these sites, phone numbers, companies, or
products beyond the life of this book.

Interior design: Laura Kashner and Emily Ghattas

ISBN 978-1-4002-3122-5 (HC)
ISBN 978-1-4002-3136-2 (eBook)

Printed in Malaysia
25 26 27 28 29 COS 11 10 9 8 7 6 5 4 3 2

To my younger (much taller) brother, Brett. I don't know why you got all the chef genes from Mom and Dad (lucky), but I sure do admire the way you love and feed your family with your entire heart. I'm so proud of you and am cheering you on always.

Written in honor of my grandmother, Frances. She loved hosting dinner parties and always set the fanciest tables—with white linen tablecloths, a full spread of silver, and beautiful porcelain china. She knew the magic of an evening was multifaceted, found not just on the plate, but also in the precise press of the tablecloth, in the twinkle of lights dimmed just so, and in the feelings of warmth and welcome in the air. Her love for hospitality lives on in us.

Contents

my mom

my mom's lasagna

A Note from Emily

They say authors write the books they need to read. And if that isn't true with this cookbook, I don't know what is. My name is Emily. I'm an entrepreneur, an author, a wife, and a mom to three school-age kids (Brady and twins Tyler and Caroline). Our lives are, to say the least, full and busy.

By trade, I'm an expert at organizing and simplifying the complicated parts of life—I created the best-selling Simplified Planner® and accompanying line of organizational tools in 2008. But one part of our family life has always been more challenging than all the rest: meals.

You see, my family wants to eat three times a day. Three! And sometimes more. As someone who doesn't necessarily enjoy making a giant mess in the kitchen or following complicated recipes most of my family won't eat anyway, cooking and meal planning are the parts of mom life I enjoy the least. This was hard and complicated when my kids were small and home all the time. But it is exponentially harder now that they are involved in sports and other activities outside of school.

I'm here to tell you there is hope. Whether you are a young adult trying to figure out what to feed yourself or you're a mom of children going in twelve different directions all day, this book is for you.

This frustration all changed for me a few years ago when I decided to stop reinventing the wheel every day. Instead of trying new recipes on busy weeknights or planning for multistep, million-ingredient meals on busy evenings—or wondering at three o'clock on a hectic Tuesday afternoon what I was going to make for dinner—I made a list of my go-to meals and decided to stick to them. These meals are the ones that just work. They're satisfying, stupid easy to make, and family approved.

Side note: "stupid easy" is my most favorite term of endearment when it comes to recipes. Stupid easy is better than regular easy. It means you have to use very little brainpower to successfully get your family from point A (hungry) to point B (fed).

What follows in this book is a very pretty presentation of my family's go-tos. I've gathered these over forty-two years of life, including fourteen years of motherhood, from friends, family, and happy accidents in the kitchen. I can't begin to tell you how excited I am that this book has come to fruition. When the idea of a cookbook was presented to me, I looked around the room and said, "Wait, me? Walk me through this. I don't love cooking. I love feeding my family and I love our time together around the table, but sautéing and chopping and mincing . . . nope."

At that moment, this concept clicked for me. Many, many of us feel this way. We love our people, and we love good food. But still. Our lives are so very full, and if cooking isn't your interest or talent, it can be quite overwhelming.

The Simplified Cookbook is your easy guide to feeding yourself and your family three times a day. I've taken extra care to make sure most of these recipes need fewer than six ingredients and take less than fifteen minutes to prep. They can be tweaked to fit your tastes and some dietary needs, but the basic recipes are easy and delicious as they are. I can't wait to hear how this helps you simplify your time in the kitchen and gives you the time and space to enjoy meals around the table with your people.

xo,
Emily

Assumptions

This book assumes a few simple things.

You have simple ingredients. In each ingredient list, I've left off items like water, salt, pepper, and cooking spray because you have those in your kitchen and can add them to a recipe fairly easily.

You can add salt and pepper to taste. I've also left off the ingredients salt and pepper when the recipe calls for "salt and pepper to taste." This means add however much you'd like. When in doubt, start with 1/4 teaspoon and taste. You can always add more later.

You can sub ingredients in and out as you see fit. Feel free to swap in and out types of vegetables, cheese, and meats throughout this cookbook. I used to get really hung up on the idea that recipes must be cooked in precise and exact ways. It's not really as complicated as that. If you'd like to use cheddar cheese instead of mozzarella, give it a try! In the grand scheme of things, it truly doesn't matter. (This is one of the biggest lessons I have learned as I've gotten more comfortable in the kitchen.)

You can adjust to your own individual dietary needs. I've omitted labels like dairy-free and gluten-free from these recipes under the assumption that *you* are best equipped to make educated, informed decisions about what is best to feed those with specific dietary requirements or preferences.

Our prep times might be different. I've taken care to make these relatively quick and easy, and have listed approximate prep times for each recipe. However, these times may vary depending on what kitchen gadgets you use, which items you purchase premade or pre-chopped, how many children might be hanging off you while you're working in the kitchen, and innumerable other factors.

You are the chef and can get fancy when you want to. I've given you the quickest way possible to get from point A (hungry) to point B (fed). In some recipes, I've also given you ways to "make it fancy" and trust that you'll follow where your heart leads!

Sometimes you prefer the simplest way forward. For instance, in our Sheet Pan Pancakes recipe, I've recommended pancake mix instead of "from scratch" pancake ingredients. There will always be times when the long way around is the way to go, but for the sake of simplicity, we've taken an easy-breezy approach here.

Stamps of Approval

Sometimes you're in a big hurry and you just need your best friend to flip open this book, point at a page, and say, "This one." Because they know exactly what you're dealing with and what you need in that moment. The Stamps of Approval in this book are basically my version of that. As you flip through the book and see these stamps throughout, just pretend like I'm flipping to each of those pages and saying, "This one. Trust me." Below are brief descriptions of each kind of stamp.

These Stamps of Approval are not exhaustive. They do not identify every single freezer friendly meal or each and every favorite (we'd have stamps on every page if that was the case). Instead, I've used these stamps to call out the game changers and the crowd favorites. You'll also find a few personal notes from me written alongside a couple recipes as well.

 Picky Eater Approved: These recipes are tried-and-true winners with the picky eaters in my house (the little ones and the big ones). Though not all picky eaters are created equal, I can pretty much guarantee these will pass any "just try a little bite" test.

 Great for Leftovers: Cook once, eat twice? Don't mind if I do! These recipes make great leftovers exactly as they are or reheated and doctored up a little.

 Emily's Pick: While I love every single recipe in this book and will cling to this hardback as a beloved resource for the rest of my days, I do have a few favorites. I'll point those out and tell you to just trust me. Make these recipes first.

 Easy to Make Ahead: When life gets wild, we have to plan ahead. If you have some time on a weekend and you'd like to get a head start on meals for the week, give these recipes a try.

 Freezer Friendly: In the same spirit of working in advance, make a few versions of these recipes, and pop them in the freezer for a day when you need something easy.

Kitchen Notes

Make-Ahead Lunch Box Meals

Like many moms, I begin each school year Pinterest-inspired—ready to craft adorable, precious, whimsical bento boxes for my children's lunches the night before school starts. Inevitably, by the third day of school, I'm tossing bags of Cheez-Its to each kid to help round out whatever they've packed last minute. The good news is, for those of us who have "pack lunches" on our to-do lists, there is a simplified approach that will not only make your kid smile but will also give you back some of your time.

Here are a few lunch box tips to keep in your back pocket.

Consider carving out a spot in your freezer for pre-prepared lunch box mains. All the ideas below freeze well. These aren't revolutionary. But sometimes we just need our memory jogged a little to remember all the great options out there.

- Ham (or turkey)-and-cheese sandwiches
- PB&J sandwiches
- Smoothies
- Muffins
- Quesadillas
- Wraps
- Tuna sandwiches
- Bagels and cream cheese
- Pimento cheese sandwiches

When making sandwiches to freeze, place any condiments between the meat and cheese (these act as a barrier to keep the condiment from making the bread mushy).

Each item will stay fresh for about one to two months in your freezer!*

Simply transfer your item from the freezer to the lunch box the morning of. It should be thawed perfectly in time for lunch.

At a certain point, children will be able to help pack their own lunch boxes. Consider this a win! Mine know to pack four items in their lunch: a main item (like a sandwich or wrap), something salty, something sweet, and something fresh. Little ones helping to pack their own lunches is game changing.

---

* According to the U.S. Department of Agriculture, https://ask.usda.gov/s/article/How-long-does-lunch-meat-stay-fresh.

ell

Feeding Picky Eaters

I made it my mission to raise kids who are adventurous eaters. I introduced new foods as early as my pediatrician approved, shared bites of my own meals at restaurants or at home, and made sure we regularly tried foods with different textures, unique flavors, and interesting backstories. Thanks to genetics, sheer luck, and my special focus on this point, my kids will eat just about anything. Caroline will not eat watermelon (a fact we all still cannot get over), and Tyler doesn't like cold tomatoes. Otherwise, my only picky eater is . . . my husband, Bryan.

So, like many of you, I am cooking for a picky eater. Bryan is a meat-and-potatoes guy. He won't eat many vegetables (unless they're part of a traditional Caesar salad), most seafood, or any white condiments. (How one can live without ranch dressing is beyond me, but here we are. We love him anyway.)

For a few years, I tried cooking dinners that made everyone happy. I quickly learned this was nearly impossible in a family of five—someone was inevitably unhappy, and I was frustrated. Instead, I now subscribe to the 3/4 rule. My goal is to make a meal that accomplishes at least three of the four goals below.

1. Few ingredients
2. Easy to make and clean up
3. Generally wholesome and healthy-ish (to me, that means it includes some form of healthy fat, fiber, and protein)
4. Something most everyone at the table will eat (or at least try)

If you aren't constantly preparing foods your people have strange feelings about, you will emerge from dinnertime victorious. For example, Bryan will not eat broccoli. Not even if you paid him. My kids and I, however, love it. They love it roasted, covered in cheese, or raw. It's in our rotation, and if a meal includes broccoli, Bryan eats a little more of the other things, which leaves more broccoli for the kids and me. In general, I've learned that going with the flow and allowing people's tastes to be what they are is just as important as continuing to introduce new foods. In my experience, no one ever decided they liked a mushroom after you made them eat it.

Regarding this challenge, I say . . .

Pick your battles. ♡

Encouragement for the Kid-Ubering Mom

Plenty of friends set my expectations for the toddler years. There'd be unending diapers, and safety contraptions to install, and jelly on nearly every surface at all times. But no one warned me about the "in-between years." These are the years in between toddlerhood and high school—when your kids can't drive themselves yet, but also don't need you to fasten their seat belts. They are more independent, but not quite teenagers. And they're involved in literally everything because these are the years when we try *it all* to see what we like most. These are the chaotic, busy, amazing years full of what I call "Kid Ubering."

It is exactly what it sounds like. You are the Uber driver. They are the passengers. Their schedules dictate where you will drive, and you hope you will receive a five-star rating at the end of the day. You are driving All. The. Time. You are driving so much that you start to move into your car. In some bag or box system, you have snacks (because everyone is always hungry). You have socks (because someone will inevitably forget them for soccer). You have pencils (so the kids who aren't dressing in the backseat for practice can do their homework). You have wet wipes (because the aforementioned jelly situation really never ends).

Some days, you are on top of the world and feel very proud of your preparedness and forward thinking. Other days, you are stopping at CVS for overpriced trail mix and extra hair ties for ballet. Kid Ubering is not easy. Being prepared in the car (with all the necessary, just-in-case supplies) is helpful, but being prepared in the kitchen (when everyone comes pouring in the front door post-practice, sweaty and starving) is genius. Here are a few rules for being a five-star Kid Uber driver.

Meal prepping is your friend. If you're going to be cooking at home on a night like this, employ your slow cooker or Instant Pot (no, it won't explode—it's a fantastic tool for busy people).

If it's financially feasible, make your busiest night every week your take-out night. Schedule delivery of something wonderful to arrive a few minutes after you know you'll be home. Dinner: done.

Instead of stressing about what to make on activity-heavy nights, slap a tradition on it and use easy recipes that you know are winners: Pizza Fridays (order it or throw it in the oven), Grilled Cheese Night (add a thin layer of mayonnaise to the outside of the bread; trust me on this one), Pasta Night (boil some pasta, top it with whatever jarred sauce you have on hand), or Leftovers Night (especially good if the meal was a hit the first time).

Speaking of leftovers, take advantage of them. Do your kids love a particular dish? Double the recipe so you have leftovers waiting to be heated up later in the week. Add a bagged salad or some steamed veggies, and this easily can satisfy hungry kiddos and lighten your burden for the evening.

In our house, I do most of the after-school Kid Ubering, so my husband makes it home before me. Sometimes we use this opportunity to order Five Guys (bunless burgers are my jam), or my husband makes his specialty: spaghetti noodles with Rao's Homemade spaghetti sauce. Voilà.

ell

For the Woman Trying to Eat Healthy-ish

Before we dive into this topic, let me say—I have *feelings* about diet culture. Having grown in up the nineties, when every diet fad imaginable was popular, I've had a complex relationship with food. In our family, we believe all foods are good (yes, even all those sugar-coated cereals—because they're delicious). We try to eat balanced meals (with healthy fats, fibers, and protein) while enjoying more of some foods and less of others. Essentially, we don't have hard-and-fast rules on foods because my brain struggles with that. If you tell me something is totally off-limits, I immediately want it. So instead of "healthy," I like to say "healthy-ish." It just lightens the mood a little.

Personally, I feel my very best when I'm eating lots of lean proteins, plenty of veggies, and a variety of fruit. My body loves whole-food nutrition and limited processed foods. But some days, the easiest thing to get on the table is tacos. Or hamburgers. Or baked spaghetti.

This used to trip me up a lot. These days, I make sure every meal has a good veggie option and plenty of protein. The rest of the meal is fine—even if it's taco shells or pasta or a loaf of French bread. Sometimes I want to enjoy these things. Other times I'll reach for extra veggies and less of the more carb-heavy or processed foods. The best way to cater to any particular preferences, in my opinion, is to have options.

This is how we get around our resident picky eater (love you, Bryan) and how we satisfy the unique palates of three rapidly growing preteen children. There are many ways the recipes in this book can be adapted to be healthier.

Add a salad. Keep a little bit (not too much) of lettuce on hand. My favorites are baby butter lettuce and romaine. You can buy these and chop, rinse, and dry them yourself, or you can buy them pre-chopped in a bag.

Make a veggie swap. On Sundays, my husband likes to grill steaks. I usually handle the sides, which are typically a Caesar salad and baked potatoes. When I discovered a great deal on frozen steam-in-bags of broccoli at Aldi once, I stocked up. Now, while making baked potatoes for the rest of the family, I steam a bag of broccoli for myself, and for just about a dollar, I can make my very own side of loaded broccoli—broccoli topped with all the delicious things you'd normally put on a baked potato.

Substitute ingredients. If you're trying to limit carbs, consider subbing a protein pasta option. If you're watching fat levels, ground turkey can replace ground beef without most people knowing you've made the switch! Fiber-rich whole-grain bread will take a sandwich or French toast in a more health-conscious direction.

Enjoy your meal, then finish it off with fruits or veggies. Life is far too short to deprive yourself, never mind the damage diet culture has caused for so many people. Even if you're working to lose a few pounds or get healthier, you can still enjoy the tacos, pancakes, and hamburgers. Have a little, then finish up with extra veggies or fresh fruit. Eating something more carb-heavy alongside healthy fats, fiber, and protein will keep you on the right track.

Help for Morning Chaos

We've all experienced it. We pressed snooze one too many times. The dog won't come in from his morning trip outside. And someone can't find their shoes. In less than an hour, the morning routine has gone off the rails.

But wait! This can go one of two ways: Your kids can reach into the fridge, grab a high-protein breakfast burrito, pop it in the microwave, and be fed and ready to go in less than five minutes.

Or the fridge could be bare. Everyone could come unglued. And granola bars could be inhaled on the way to school.

Nothing wrong with a granola bar for breakfast, but it's no breakfast burrito, and you can't beat starting your day with some protein.

Plan for the unexpected. Because, as my dad says, if it can happen, it will. And at the most inopportune time.

This is me telling you to stock that freezer! Future you will thank past you for having the foresight (and taking the time) to prep a few things before the inevitable morning madness unfolds.

MORNING MADNESS TIPS

- Keep grab-and-go breakfast items on hand (and within small-people reach), such as Greek yogurt, protein bars, or single-serve oatmeal cups.

- Once a month, spend an hour or so making breakfast sandwiches or burritos to keep in the freezer. When you need them, simply take them out, wrap them in paper towels, and microwave for 2 minutes (or until fully warmed).

- If you're not a big breakfast eater (on weekdays, I'm not), try adding a little protein to your morning drink. I love Premier Protein added to my coffee or a scoop of vanilla protein to a smoothie.

Assembly Meals—Your New Best Friend

Some days, it's 6 p.m., I'm starving, and I just want to be able to throw a few things together to get everyone fed. Enter our superhero: assembly meals.

I know what you're thinking: *What in the world is an assembly meal?* Well, if you're like me and cooking doesn't always spark joy, I want you to know that you have options other than takeout or pizza delivery. You don't need a culinary degree or a pantry full of exotic ingredients to whip up a delicious dinner for your family. Sometimes the best meals are the ones that come together with just a few simple ingredients.

Think of assembly meals as your easiest go-tos—quick, simple, and so satisfying. These are the meals where precise measuring and extra steps go out the window, and you get your people fed by throwing together whatever ingredients you have on hand. It's all about creativity and flexibility—two words that always catch my attention.

Picture this: whatever veggies are around, a protein of your choice (hello, leftover rotisserie chicken!), some pasta, and your favorite sauce. Toss it all together in a bowl, and voilà, dinner is served. No need to stress about following a complicated recipe or spending hours making a mess in the kitchen.

In addition to these basics, I like to keep several items regularly stocked in my fridge, freezer, and pantry so I have last-minute options when I need them. These aren't our everyday meals, but they're what I reach for in a pinch. Plus, they're often a bit more affordable than fast food or takeout.

- Frozen lasagna
- Frozen chicken tenders
- Macaroni and cheese
- Frozen veggies of all sorts (steam-in-bag options are great)
- Pasta
- Spaghetti sauce

Feeding your family doesn't have to be complicated to be done well and with a lot of love. Assembly meals might be gatherings of leftovers, or they might be arrangements of charcuterie and whatever cheese and crackers you have. Essentially, assembly meals are made with the ingredients you have on hand, with the time you have, and for the people you love. Throughout each section of this cookbook, you'll find both recipes and assembly meals to choose from.

The next time you're feeling overwhelmed by the thought of cooking dinner, remember that a delicious meal can be simply assembled in no time.

ell

So You Want to Love Cooking, but You Just Don't

Let's talk about something near and dear to our hearts (and stomachs). I know cooking isn't everyone's cup of tea. In fact, some of us would rather do just about anything else than spend hours in the kitchen after a busy day tending to #alltheotherthings. But wouldn't it be nice to actually enjoy whipping up a meal for your family without feeling like you're auditioning for a cooking show? Trust me, I get it.

If you're nodding along, thinking, *Yes, Emily, that's me!* here are a few ideas that might just help you find the same measure of kitchen joy they've given me.

Focus on simple recipes. If you've picked up this cookbook, you're on the right track. Discovering a few go-to meals your family loves and you enjoy cooking is game changing. Opt for recipes with just a few ingredients and easy-to-follow instructions. Keep it straightforward to reduce stress and make cooking less of a chore.

Make a meal plan. Take a few minutes each week to plan your meals—at least your dinners. Depending on your circumstances, you might be able to count on, for example, one night out, one night of leftovers, and one on-the-go night with takeout. That leaves you with just four dinners to map out. It will take a few minutes to plan things out, but knowing what you'll be cooking ahead of time can save you from last-minute scrambling and decision fatigue.

Cook in batches. Utilize batch-cooking techniques to prepare larger quantities of food at once. This can save time throughout the week and provide ready-made meals for busy days. You can batch-cook quinoa, rice, vegetables (potatoes, carrots, broccoli, cauliflower, brussels sprouts), and protein like chicken or beef.

Get the family involved. Turn meal preparation into a family activity by assigning tasks to each family member. This is a great opportunity for teaching moments. Not only does sharing the responsibilities lighten your load, but it also fosters quality time and teaches valuable cooking skills.

Experiment with one-pot meals. Simplify your cooking process by making one-pot meals like soups, stews, or casseroles. They require less cleanup, and often you'll have leftovers for the next day.

Embrace convenience. If it fits into your budget, don't hesitate to use precut vegetables, frozen onions or minced garlic, canned beans, or rotisserie chicken to streamline cooking. These convenience foods can significantly cut down on cooking time and effort. Also, scour Amazon for finds that make cooking easier (veggie choppers forever!).

Cook what you like. Here's a game changer—cook what you actually like to eat. No more baking salmon and spinach when it doesn't even sound appetizing to you. Curate a list of go-to meals that are sure to make bellies and hearts happy.

Romanticize the process. Enjoy the rhythmic chopping of vegetables, the sizzle of ingredients in a pan, and the aroma of spices filling your kitchen. Play your favorite music, listen to an audiobook with headphones, light a scented candle, or pour yourself your favorite beverage while cooking. Transforming your kitchen into a cozy, inviting space can make the experience more enjoyable.

Remember, finding joy in cooking doesn't mean you have to become a gourmet chef overnight. It's about discovering what works for you and your family, redefining what a great meal looks like, and finding moments of satisfaction in the kitchen, even on the busiest of days.

Freezer Meals for Big Life Events

Meal prep can be especially helpful when you're anticipating an impending busy season—a baby's arrival, long-term medical treatment, or just an insanely busy couple of weeks or months. Having a plan in place for feeding your family can be a game changer. And guess what? Freezer meals are about to become your new best friend.

So, what exactly are freezer meals? Think of them as your secret weapon in the battle against mealtime chaos. These are meals you prep ahead of time, stash in the freezer, then pull out whenever you need a quick and easy dinner solution.

Let's break it down. Here's how to make a big batch of freezer meals all at once.

Choose your recipes. Start by selecting recipes that freeze well and are easy to reheat. Think hearty soups, stews, casseroles, and chili—anything that can be cooked low and slow or quickly in a pressure cooker.

Gather ingredients. Make a list of everything you'll need for each recipe, and then hit the grocery store to stock up. Consider doubling or even tripling recipes to maximize your efforts and ensure you have plenty of meals on hand. While you're there, be sure to pick up freezer-safe resealable bags and markers for storing and labeling.

Get to work. Set aside a block of time—several hours on a weekend perhaps—to prep your freezer meals. Chop veggies, brown meat, assemble casseroles—whatever needs to be done to get your meals ready for the freezer.

Pack it up. Once your meals are prepped, portion them into freezer-safe resealable bags. Label everything with the name of the dish, the date, and the cooking instructions so you know exactly what you're working with when mealtime rolls around.

Freeze! Lay your meals flat in the freezer if you can (to save space)—making sure to leave enough room for air circulation.

When it's time to cook, simply pull a meal out of the freezer, dump it into your slow cooker or Instant Pot, and let the magic happen. No fuss, no stress—just yummy, easy meals your family will love. With a little planning and prep work, you can ensure that your family stays happily well-fed and nourished when life gets hectic.

Why Dinnertime Matters

I've never been able to fully throw in the towel on cooking. Mostly because I'm in charge of three small humans who need to eat multiple times a day, but also because I genuinely want to grow to enjoy the process. My appreciation for cooking is growing—even if slowly—but what keeps me going is remembering why I'm making the mess and putting forth all the effort in the first place. Because dinnertime matters.

Dinnertime is about more than just filling hungry bellies; it's about nourishing our bodies and our hearts. It is a time for us to come together as a family, set aside the craziness of the day, and connect. As a busy professional, wife, mother, and more, I struggle daily to balance work, life, and family. And most days around 5 p.m., the last thing I want to do is spend hours in the kitchen preparing complicated meals. I crave simplicity, efficiency, and the opportunity to unwind with my people.

In our fast-paced, activity-packed, nonstop world, finding moments to connect can be hard. Dinnertime offers a sacred slice of time for us to set aside distractions and focus on each other—whether we're seated around a beautifully set table with main dishes, sides, and dessert or standing around the kitchen, leaning against the cabinets, stuffing our faces with pizza that was just delivered. These moments of togetherness matter.

By embracing simplicity in the kitchen, we can create space for that togetherness to happen. Added bonus? We all get fed. Happy bellies. Happy hearts. Embracing the duality of not necessarily loving cooking but also really enjoying our people is how we make room for both.

Try a 'round-the-table conversation starter like asking each person to name a high and a low from the day.

Perfectionism Has No Place in Your Kitchen

When it comes to meal planning and cooking, perfectionism is a problem many busy women face. As a recovering perfectionist, for years I defined "a great dinner at home" as a brand-new recipe, created entirely from scratch, presented exquisitely, and given five stars by everyone at the table. This was my expectation until I realized the truth behind the phrase "perfect is the enemy of good." Perfection can absolutely suck the joy out of everything.

So when it comes to meal planning and cooking, remember that perfection is not the goal. While it's natural to want to check every box with every single meal—nutritious, beautiful, and universally adored—it's so important to give ourselves permission to let go of unrealistic expectations. Instead of aiming for gourmet dinners every night, focus on creating meals that are nourishing, satisfying, and practical for your family's needs. It's okay to rely on simple recipes, shortcuts, and sometimes even convenience foods—what matters most is that your family is fed and together.

Instead of striving for perfection with each meal, strive for a happy dinnertime experience in whatever way that applies to you and your family. For example, when I realized that making fancy bento box lunches for my children to take to school every day wasn't worth my sanity, I started focusing on other ways I could make them smile when they opened their lunch boxes. I began buying cute paper napkins when I found them on sale (I have quite the collection now!). I write lunch box notes to tell them I love them and am thinking of them. When they were younger, I used cookie cutters to turn their PB&Js into dinosaurs. I even started buying unique and fun types of mini-desserts or treats for them to try with their plain old ham sandwiches, chips, and grapes.

I think it's important to identify where your joy resides and invest your time there. That's where we shine the most. You cook Thanksgiving dinner; I'll set a killer table. Find your joy in the kitchen and chase it. Love baking and listening to audiobooks? Go for it. The bake sale awaits. Love slow-cooking barbecue all day and making your house smell amazing? Forget the salmon and spinach; barbecue it is! You do you. Don't let perfection be the enemy of good.

good > perfect

Rely on a Perpetual Grocery List

It sometimes seems like just as I finish one trip to the grocery store, it's time to go back. But what if I told you there's a simple solution to this never-ending cycle? Enter the magic of keeping a perpetual grocery list.

A perpetual grocery list is exactly what it sounds like—a running list of items you regularly need to buy, updated as needed and kept handy for whenever it's time to hit the store. It's like having your own personal assistant reminding you of what you need without the hassle of starting from scratch every week.

Instead of racking your brain trying to remember the staples you like to keep on hand or scrambling to jot down items as you run out the door, simply consult your list and add anything that's missing. No more starting your list from scratch each week! This saves time and mental energy, leaving you more room to focus on other important tasks.

So how do you create and maintain a perpetual grocery list? Start by taking inventory of your pantry, fridge, and freezer to identify items you use regularly, staples like milk, bread, eggs, produce, rice, pasta, and canned goods. Keep your list somewhere easily accessible—whether it's a notepad on the fridge or a note-taking app on your phone—and add to it as needed whenever you notice something running low or think of something your family needs consistently.

On the opposite page is a wonderful starting place for your perpetual grocery list. Add or remove based on your preferences.

Perpetual Grocery List

PRODUCE

- ☑ Apples
- ☑ Bananas
- ☑ Berries
- ☑ Carrots
- ☑ Garlic
- ☑ Lemons
- ☑ Lettuce
- ☑ Potatoes
- ☑ Yellow onions

DAIRY + EGGS

- ☑ Butter
- ☑ Cream cheese
- ☑ Eggs
- ☑ Greek yogurt
- ☑ Half-and-half
- ☑ Heavy whipping cream
- ☑ Milk
- ☑ Shredded cheese
- ☑ Sliced cheese

PROTEIN

- ☑ Chicken breasts
- ☑ Chicken thighs
- ☑ Chuck roast
- ☑ Deli meat
- ☑ Ground beef
- ☑ Salmon

GRAINS + BREADS

- ☑ Bread
- ☑ Old-fashioned oats
- ☑ Pasta
- ☑ Rice (steam-in-bags)
- ☑ Tortillas

PANTRY STAPLES

- ☑ Beans
- ☑ Chicken broth
- ☑ Flour, all purpose
- ☑ Honey
- ☑ Jelly
- ☑ Maple syrup
- ☑ Olive oil
- ☑ Peanut butter
- ☑ Sugar
- ☑ Vinegar

CONDIMENTS

- ☑ BBQ Sauce
- ☑ Dijon mustard
- ☑ Hot sauce
- ☑ Ketchup
- ☑ Mayonnaise
- ☑ Mustard
- ☑ Olives
- ☑ Pickles
- ☑ Soy sauce

SPICES

- ☑ Chili powder
- ☑ Cumin
- ☑ Garlic powder
- ☑ Onion powder
- ☑ Oregano
- ☑ Paprika
- ☑ Parsley
- ☑ Pepper
- ☑ Salt

SNACKS

- ☑ Crackers
- ☑ Granola bars
- ☑ Nuts
- ☑ Popcorn
- ☑ Pretzels

HOUSEHOLD ITEMS

- ☑ Cleaning supplies
- ☑ Freezer-safe bags
- ☑ Laundry detergent
- ☑ Paper towels
- ☑ Toilet paper

BEVERAGES

- ☑ Coffee
- ☑ Orange juice

What Doesn't Really Matter in the Kitchen

Let's chat about something super important: the cooking techniques and teachings that really don't matter in the kitchen, especially when you're juggling a million things at once. Because most of the time, getting dinner on the table is priority; being perfect and exact in your process doesn't really matter in the end. Here are a few techniques you can toss out the window and still get beautiful, delicious meals on the table.

Obsessing over knife skills. Sure, it's great if you can chop an onion like a pro, but you don't need perfect knife skills to make a delicious meal. As long as your veggies are roughly the same size, they'll cook evenly. Don't stress over precision—just chop safely and get cooking!

Getting fancy with plating. While it's fun to make your dishes look pretty, you don't need to spend hours arranging microgreens or drizzling sauces *just-so* across your plate. Your family won't care if their dinner looks like a work of art—they just want something tasty to eat. Focus on flavor over aesthetics, and save the fancy plating for special occasions.

Sticking strictly to recipes. Recipes are more like guidelines than strict rules. (This threw me for an absolute loop when I realized it; I always thought you had to be exact!) Baking requires a different level of precision to create the desired end result, but when you're cooking, feel free to improvise. Make substitutions based on what you have on hand or your family's preferences. Cooking should be flexible and fun, not stressful and rigid. Trust your instincts and get creative in the kitchen. If you're like me, this will take practice. Give yourself permission to play.

Sweating exact internal temps and cooking times. Sure, recipes might say to cook a dish for twenty minutes, but every oven is different, and personal preferences vary. Use cooking times as a rough estimate and rely on visual cues, like golden-brown edges or bubbling sauce, to know when your food is done.

Insisting on fresh ingredients. While fresh ingredients are nice, they're not always practical—especially when you're busy. Don't feel guilty about using canned, frozen, or prepackaged ingredients. They're convenient, budget friendly, and just as tasty. Embrace the shortcuts and save yourself some time and hassle.

Remember, cooking is about nourishing your family and enjoying the process. Don't let unnecessary rules or techniques stress you out. Keep it simple, trust your instincts, and enjoy learning as you go.

Gadgets, Gizmos, and Little Luxuries

I absolutely love finding unnecessary necessities to make life easier, particularly in the kitchen. Below are a few items I keep in my kitchen for added convenience and ultimately less time prepping.

- **Veggie chopper:** Veggie choppers are a game changer, especially if you don't want your mascara to run while chopping onions. Simply cut veggies into medium-size pieces, lay on the blades, and press the lid down. Voilà! Perfectly cut veggies, all the same size, in just seconds.

- **Meat chopper:** Long gone are the days of trying to break up ground beef with a wooden spoon. Meat choppers break the meat up with ease and help it cook faster.

- **Scraper:** I chop my veggies on a wooden cutting board across from my stove. So when I need to transfer the chopped stuff to the pot, I often drop something on the floor. The dog loves it, but I don't love the mess. Scrapers help you pick it all up and get it where it needs to be.

- **Meat thermometer:** Fear chicken no more. Simply insert the meat thermometer to check the doneness.

- **Oil mister:** Traditional cooking sprays can contain unwanted additives, while store-bought aerosol oil sprays can be expensive and wasteful. An oil mister allows you to create your own cooking spray using your favorite oil, giving you control over the ingredients and portion size.

- **Avocado slicer:** If you love avocados but struggle with slicing and pitting them, an avocado slicer is your new best friend. It allows you to effortlessly cut, pit, and slice avocados with precision, making it easier to enjoy this delicious fruit in salads, sandwiches, and more.

- **Precut foil and parchment paper:** Precut foil and parchment paper eliminate the need (and hassle) of measuring and cutting from a roll. With perfect-sized sheets, they make cooking and baking just a little easier and more enjoyable.

- **Air fryer and slow cooker liners:** Precut, ready to go, nonstick. Need I say more?

- **Kitchen shears:** These specialty scissors allow you to chop herbs, vegetables, meat, and more while minimizing mess and cleanup.

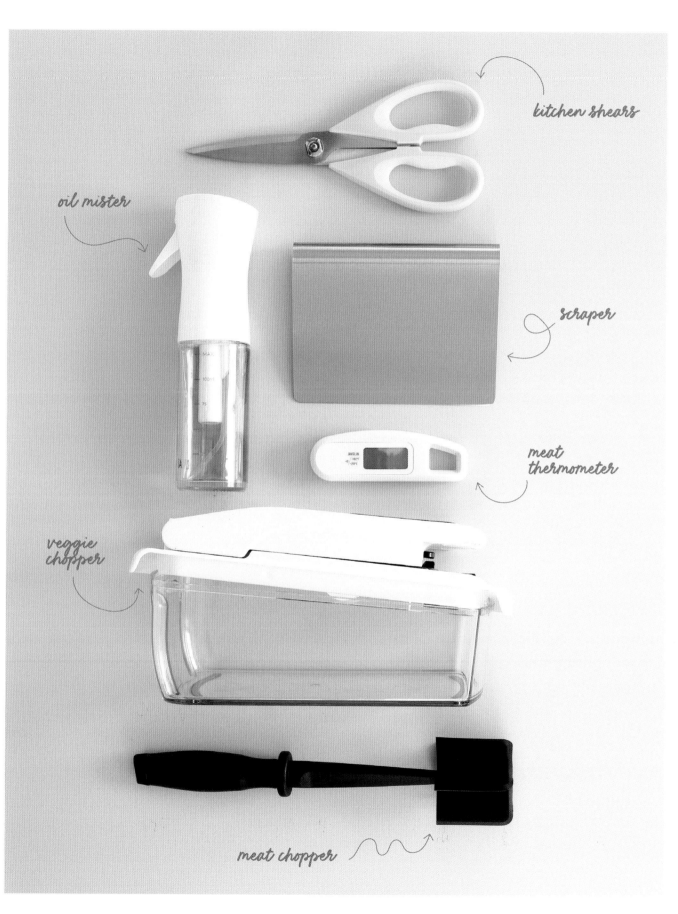

kitchen shears

oil mister

scraper

meat thermometer

veggie chopper

meat chopper

Nourishing Your Body

Have you ever felt that managing a busy life and getting meals onto the table means choosing between feeding your family something healthy *or* something convenient? I know I've felt that way. Though the term *healthy* can be defined different ways depending on who you ask and what their priorities are, here are a few universal tips for making simple, convenient meals while feeding your family foods that nourish their bodies.

When grocery shopping, prioritize organic for the Dirty Dozen.* Buying organic produce can be expensive. The Environmental Working Group's Dirty Dozen list identifies the top twelve fruits and vegetables each year with the highest pesticide residues when grown conventionally. To minimize exposure to pesticides, consider prioritizing organic options for these twelve foods:

- Apples
- Celery
- Cherries
- Grapes
- Kale
- Nectarines
- Peaches
- Pears
- Potatoes
- Spinach
- Strawberries
- Tomatoes

Eat real food. Focus on shopping the perimeter of the grocery store and eating foods that come from the earth, in lots of different colors. This ensures that you're getting the vitamins, minerals, and other nutrients necessary for overall health and well-being. Choose whole foods over processed options.

Choose oils wisely. While some oils have proven to be good for the heart and to fight inflammation in the body, others can cause inflammation, which has been linked to numerous diseases. Prioritize oils high in monounsaturated and polyunsaturated fats like olive oil, avocado oil, and some nut oils while limiting oils high in omega-6 fatty acids, such as vegetable oils, sunflower oil, and soybean oil.

*The 2024 Dirty Dozen™, ewg.org.

Additional Tips

Find a favorite olive oil. Not all olive oils are the same. If you have time and have an olive oil shop near you, pay them a visit. Many olive oil shops will allow you to taste their various offerings. Personally, I like a very mild olive oil for cooking and for dressings. More pungent, strong-flavored olive oils throw off a recipe if you ask me. Find one you like and stick with it.

Get to know your spices. I think it's helpful to understand and know your spices. One afternoon, when you have some uninterrupted free time, get out all your spices, sit down, and get to know them. Smell each of them. Taste them. Get a good loaf of French bread and some olive oil, and play around with the spices, tasting them on the bread with the oil. This will sharpen your instincts regarding which spices taste good with which foods.

Don't let chicken freak you out. I had salmonella as a child, no thanks to a contaminated jar of baby food. Though I was just a baby, I've grown up with a healthy fear of raw chicken. For years I served chicken very well done (read: DRY) or not at all. Enter the meat thermometer. Now I simply check that my chicken has reached 165 degrees internally, and I know it's fully cooked.

Fresh herbs are better, but you don't need a garden if you don't want one. In your fridge, keep small cups of store-bought fresh herbs you use often. They stay fresh longer than if you leave them in the plastic containers and taste better than dried herbs in some recipes. Basil and parsley are two good ones to have on hand.

Watch the broiler. Minding the broiler is just one of those things you don't know *until you know*. Until you've set an entire pan of nachos on fire, you just don't know how hot that broiler can get and how fast. Whenever I use my broiler, whether it's to melt cheese quickly or add a little extra crispiness, I always crack the oven door and stand right in front of the oven, watching and waiting for my food to be crisped just right.

Breakfast

Breakfast

Easy Quiche

Quiches are so yummy and can be customized a number of ways. I love serving quiche at brunch or delivering one to a friend who's just had a baby or is going through a hard time. This quiche is quick, simple, and bakes in no time. You can use a premade piecrust placed into your own pie plate or the kind that's already in a disposable metal pan to save a dish. You can even sneak in some chopped spinach if you'd like.

 PREP TIME
10 minutes

 COOK TIME
60 minutes

 SERVINGS
8

INGREDIENTS

- 1 (9-inch) premade piecrust
- 4 eggs
- 1 cup half-and-half
- 1 cup diced ham
- 1 cup shredded cheddar cheese
- Optional: 1 cup baby spinach, finely chopped

DIRECTIONS

1. Preheat oven to 375 degrees.
2. If you're using a crust that is not in a tin, press the crust into a greased 9-inch pie plate. Remove excess dough from edges.
3. In a mixing bowl, whisk together eggs and half-and-half. Fold in ham and cheese, and spinach, (if using).
4. Pour egg mixture into pie plate.
5. Bake for 60 minutes or until center is firm.
6. Remove from oven. Add salt and pepper to taste.
7. Let cool for 10 minutes before serving.

✳ **PRO TIP**

Buy premade piecrust and pre-diced ham.

Hashbrown Bake

Breakfast bakes are awesome because you can assemble them ahead of time and leave them in the fridge until they're ready to be cooked. My family loves this simple egg bake for a protein-packed breakfast. You can even freeze individual pieces for a heat-and-eat option. If you want to sneak in some veggies, you can sauté chopped bell peppers and yellow onion in a little olive oil in the same pan you brown your sausage in, then add them to the eggs when you add the cheese.

PREP TIME
10 minutes

COOK TIME
50 minutes

SERVINGS
8 to 12

INGREDIENTS

- 1 lb ground sausage
- 9 eggs
- 1 cup whole milk
- 2 cups shredded cheddar cheese
- 1 (20 oz) bag shredded hash brown potatoes
- Optional: 1/2 bell pepper, diced
- Optional: 1 yellow onion, chopped

DIRECTIONS

1. Preheat oven to 375 degrees. Spray a 9 x 13-inch baking dish with nonstick cooking spray.
2. Brown the ground sausage in a skillet over medium heat. If you are using optional veggies, add them to the skillet and cook for a couple more minutes. Remove from heat.
3. Whisk eggs and milk in a bowl, then add to baking dish.
4. Stir sausage, cheese, and hash browns into the egg mixture in the baking dish.
5. Bake for 50 minutes.
6. Remove from oven and let cool for 10 minutes before serving.

Banana Pancakes

Does anyone else start singing the Jack Johnson song when you see these words? Just me? These easy pancakes were one of my oldest's favorites when he was smaller. Now that he's a teenager (gracious), he still loves them just as much.

PREP TIME
10 minutes

COOK TIME
15 minutes

SERVINGS
4

INGREDIENTS

- Butter, for the pan
- 4 overripe bananas
- 4 eggs
- 1 cup all-purpose flour
- 1/2 tsp baking powder
- Optional: sliced bananas, maple syrup, powdered sugar

DIRECTIONS

1. Grease a pan with butter, and heat on medium.
2. In a mixing bowl, mash bananas with a fork.
3. Stir in eggs, flour, and baking powder until just mixed.
4. Pour 1/4 cup batter into pan. Press and shape into a circle (batter will be thick). Cook until brown, about 2 minutes. Flip to brown on the other side, about 1 minute.
5. Serve with sliced bananas, maple syrup, or powdered sugar for a sweet breakfast.

Classic French Toast

Nothing hits the happy button quite like classic French toast. It's so easy to make that you can even get your kids involved. Top with powdered sugar, syrup, or your favorite berries for a delicious Sunday breakfast.

PREP TIME
10 minutes

COOK TIME
15 minutes

SERVINGS
4

INGREDIENTS

- 4 eggs
- 1 tsp vanilla extract
- 1 tsp cinnamon
- 1 cup milk
- Butter, for the pan
- 8 slices bread
- Optional: maple syrup, powdered sugar, berries

DIRECTIONS

1. Whisk eggs, vanilla, cinnamon, and milk in a shallow dish.
2. Heat a pan or griddle over medium heat, and slide butter across it as it gets warm.
3. Dip both sides of a slice of bread into egg mixture, then add to the hot pan.
4. Cook each slice about 2 minutes per side. Remove from pan. Repeat with remaining bread slices, adding more butter to the pan as needed.
5. Top with powdered sugar, maple syrup, and/or berries.

Egg Bites

I constantly find myself trying to get more protein into my kids. Egg bites are one of the easiest ways I've found. These are also a great way to use up any leftovers you have on hand—or to put that bag of spinach about to expire to good use. My kids think they're extra great served with ketchup, of course.

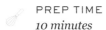 **PREP TIME**
10 minutes

 **COOK TIME**
20 minutes

 **SERVINGS**
12 egg bites

INGREDIENTS

- 8 eggs
- 1/4 cup milk
- 1/2 cup baby spinach
- 1 cup diced ham
- 1/2 cup shredded cheddar cheese

DIRECTIONS

1. Preheat oven to 350 degrees. Spray a 12-cup muffin pan with nonstick cooking spray.
2. Whisk eggs and milk in a bowl. Add salt and pepper to taste.
3. Chop spinach. Divide spinach, ham, and cheese evenly into muffin cups.
4. Pour an equal amount of egg mixture into each cup.
5. Bake for 20 minutes.

 PRO TIP

Buy pre-diced ham.

Pumpkin Muffins

The nostalgia of pumpkin muffins is very real for me. I can smell these, warm and straight from the oven, just writing this! Because this recipe calls for a box of cake mix, these are a little more of a dessert-type breakfast. But who doesn't love a treat every now and then, especially on a cool fall morning?

PREP TIME

10 minutes

COOK TIME

20 minutes

SERVINGS

2 dozen muffins

INGREDIENTS

- 1 (15.25 oz) box spiced cake mix
- 1 (15 oz) can pure pumpkin
- 2 Tbsp brown sugar

DIRECTIONS

1. Preheat oven to 350 degrees. Spray two 12-cup muffin tins with nonstick cooking spray.
2. Mix cake mix and pumpkin together. Divide batter evenly among muffin tins.
3. Sprinkle brown sugar on top of each muffin.
4. Bake for 18 to 20 minutes, or until a toothpick inserted in the middle of a muffin comes out clean.

Slow Cooker Apple Oatmeal

Thank goodness for slow cookers. I love to start these overnight oats after supper, while cleaning the kitchen. I turn on the slow cooker just before bed (I love using the auto shut-off feature so these don't overcook). The smell when you wake up in the morning is so yummy and cozy. These are great for cold winter mornings and getting the kids out the door quickly. Add chopped nuts, raisins, or a pinch of salt if you're feeling fancy! Also, try a slow cooker liner—your arm muscles will thank you later when you're not scraping cooked oatmeal off the sides.

PREP TIME
10 minutes

COOK TIME
6 hours

SERVINGS
4 to 6

INGREDIENTS

- 1 cup steel-cut oats
- 4 cups milk
- 2 apples
- 1/4 cup brown sugar, plus extra for sprinkling
- 1/2 tsp cinnamon
- Optional: sliced apple, to top

DIRECTIONS

1. Spray a slow cooker with nonstick cooking spray or line with a slow cooker liner.
2. Peel and chop apples into large chunks.
3. Mix oats, milk, apples, brown sugar, and cinnamon in slow cooker.
4. Cover and cook on low for 6 to 8 hours or until liquid is mostly absorbed. Be careful not to overcook.
5. In the morning, spoon oatmeal into bowls, sprinkle with brown sugar, and serve.

Swap in blueberries, bananas, or peanut butter for a twist!

Sunday Morning Casserole

This recipe, shared on my friend Annie's blog, *Home of Malones*, is our favorite Sunday morning breakfast. We love it so much, in fact, that we have it on Christmas morning. It's so easy to prepare that my kids can make it on their own.

 PREP TIME
10 minutes

 COOK TIME
30 minutes

 SERVINGS
8 to 12

INGREDIENTS

- 1 (8 oz) can crescent roll dough
- 1 lb ground sausage or diced cooked ham
- 9 eggs
- 1 1/2 cups shredded cheddar cheese

DIRECTIONS

1. Preheat oven to 350 degrees. Spray a 9 x 13-inch baking dish with nonstick cooking spray.
2. Unroll crescent dough in bottom of baking dish.
3. If using sausage, brown it in a skillet over medium heat until it is cooked through, then drain it and place it on top of dough. If using ham, place it on top of the dough.
4. Whisk eggs, then pour them on top of the sausage and dough.
5. Top with shredded cheese.
6. Bake for 30 minutes.

 PRO TIP

Try the Jimmy Dean Maple Premium Pork Sausage. It is *chef's kiss*.

Sheet Pan Pancakes

Pancakes are so much fun to make and even more fun to eat. But sometimes, my pancake-making skills can't quite keep up with my family's pancake-eating skills. Making pancakes one by one is fine, but making pancakes on a baking sheet is pure genius. You can even use different toppings on different areas of the baking sheet for different types of pancakes. For the pancake mix, we like Bisquick.

 PREP TIME
10 minutes

 COOK TIME
15 minutes

 SERVINGS
4 to 6

a great dish to feed a crowd

INGREDIENTS

- 4 cups pancake mix
- 4 eggs
- 2 cups milk
- Maple syrup, for topping
- Optional mix-ins: blueberries, diced strawberries, chocolate chips, bananas

DIRECTIONS

1. Preheat oven to 425 degrees. Spray a large rimmed baking sheet with nonstick cooking spray.
2. In a bowl, mix pancake mix, eggs, and milk.
3. Pour pancake mix into baking sheet.
4. Add mix-ins on top of the pancake mix.
5. Bake for 15 minutes.
6. Remove pan from oven, slice, and top with maple syrup.

The World's Best Scrambled Eggs

Who doesn't love a big helping of scrambled eggs? I've been taught several methods to arrive at the perfect scrambled egg, but this one is my favorite. Not only is the end result full of protein, but the eggs are creamy, fluffy, and delicious.

 **PREP TIME**
10 minutes

 **COOK TIME**
5 minutes

 SERVINGS
2

INGREDIENTS

- 3 eggs
- 1/4 cup cottage cheese
- 1 Tbsp butter

DIRECTIONS

1. Warm a skillet over medium-low heat. Crack eggs into a medium bowl. Whisk thoroughly using a fork.
2. Add butter to warm skillet, and let it melt to entirely coat the bottom. Add cottage cheese to the bowl.
3. Add whisked eggs to the pan, then a pinch of salt and the cottage cheese.
4. With a heat-safe spatula, move eggs around the pan.
5. Once eggs are no longer liquid (shiny but not wet), remove them from heat. The eggs will continue cooking, so depending on how you like them, you could plate them immediately or wait a few minutes.

 PRO TIP

Take your eggs out of the fridge 10 to 15 minutes before cooking them. This allows the eggs to come closer to room temperature and makes them easier to whisk.

Biscuits & Gravy

Quintessentially Southern, biscuits and gravy is my favorite weekend breakfast food. It is super easy to make, and the delicious smell of biscuits baking will have even your teenager waking up early to partake. If you don't want to make your own gravy, there are good gravy mixes. We like Pioneer Peppered Gravy Mix.

 PREP TIME
10 minutes

 COOK TIME
20 minutes

 SERVINGS
8

INGREDIENTS

- 1 (16.3 oz) can buttermilk biscuits
- 1 lb ground sausage
- 1/4 cup all-purpose flour
- 2 cups milk

DIRECTIONS

1. Preheat oven according to the instructions on the biscuits can.
2. Spray an 8 x 8-inch baking dish with nonstick cooking spray. Put biscuits in the pan and bake according to the directions.
3. While biscuits bake, brown sausage in a skillet until it is cooked through. Do not drain.
4. Add flour to pan and stir until it is just starting to brown.
5. Whisk in 1 1/2 cups of the milk, stirring constantly. Add more milk as needed until the desired consistency is reached (you may not need all 2 cups). Remove from heat.
6. Top baked biscuits with the sausage gravy and serve.

Breakfast
Assembly Meals

assembly meal:	a quick, easy dish made by combining ready-to-use ingredients with little or no cooking. see also: lifesaver.

Overnight Oats

INGREDIENTS

- 2 cups old-fashioned oats
- 2 cups milk
- 4 Tbsp brown sugar
- 4 Tbsp peanut butter
- 1 1/2 Tbsp chia seeds
- Optional: nuts, dried fruit, fresh fruit

DIRECTIONS

1. Add oats, milk, brown sugar, peanut butter, and chia seeds to a mixing bowl and stir to combine.
2. Divide mixture evenly between 4 mason jars.
3. Refrigerate overnight or for 6 to 8 hours.
4. Stir, top with any nuts, dried fruit, or fresh fruit you'd like, and enjoy!

* PRO TIP
You can always omit the chia seeds if you'd like and increase or decrease the amount of milk based on the texture you prefer.

Easy Breakfast Sandwiches

INGREDIENTS

- 3 to 4 Tbsp butter, softened
- 6 English muffins
- 6 slices cheddar cheese
- 6 eggs
- 6 slices deli ham

DIRECTIONS

1. Preheat oven to 375 degrees.
2. Butter the insides of the English muffins. Place them on a baking sheet, buttered side up.
3. Top one half of each English muffin with one slice of cheese.
4. Bake for 3 minutes. Remove from the oven.
5. In a skillet over medium heat, scramble eggs until they are firm and set. Divide them among the cheese-topped English muffins.
6. Fold and place one slice of ham on top of the eggs on each English muffin half.
7. Top with the other half of each muffin.

Strawberry Banana Smoothies

INGREDIENTS

- 1 cup frozen strawberries
- 1 banana
- 1 cup milk
- 1/2 cup strawberry Greek yogurt

DIRECTIONS

1. Add berries, banana, milk, and yogurt to your blender and blend until smooth.

Baby Donuts

INGREDIENTS

- 2 to 4 cups vegetable oil, for deep frying
- 1 (16.3 oz) can flaky biscuits
- Powdered sugar, for topping

DIRECTIONS

1. Pour oil into a saucepan over medium-high heat (you want the oil to reach about 350 degrees). To make sure your oil is ready for the dough, stick the end of a wooden spoon into it. If bubbles form around all edges, it's ready. If not, it's not warm enough yet.
2. Separate biscuits and cut them into quarters.
3. Roll biscuit pieces into balls.
4. A few at a time, gently place balls into hot oil (careful, it may splatter). Allow one side to get golden brown before gently flipping each donut, about 1 to 2 minutes per side.
5. Once donuts are golden brown on both sides, remove from oil and place on a paper towel to drain. Top with powdered sugar while still warm.

* PRO TIP
You can also use a fondue pot for this recipe. Simply add your oil to the pot and set the temperature to 350 degrees. Once the oil is hot, begin gently dropping in your donuts. Also, if you're in the mood for cinnamon, swap the powdered sugar for a little cinnamon and sugar as your topping.

Avocado Toast

INGREDIENTS

- 4 slices bread
- 2 avocados
- Everything bagel seasoning
- Optional: radishes, pine nuts, cilantro

DIRECTIONS

1. Toast the bread. If you're cooking for more than one, toast the bread in the oven at 350 degrees on a baking sheet for 4 to 6 minutes, then flip the slices and return to the oven for 4 to 5 more minutes (the timing will depend on your oven).
2. Slice open and pit avocados. Scoop the avocado into a bowl and mash.
3. Spread mashed avocado over toast and top it with everything bagel seasoning.
4. Add any other toppings you like.

* PRO TIP
A friend of ours, George Lazi (owner and chef of the amazing George Bistro Bar), tops his avocado toast with sliced radishes, pine nuts, and cilantro. It's delicious! Be as fancy as you like.

Breakfast Burritos

INGREDIENTS

- 1 lb ground sausage
- 6 eggs
- 6 to 8 tortillas
- 1 1/2 cups shredded cheddar cheese
- Optional: salsa, green onions, and cilantro for topping

DIRECTIONS

1. Brown sausage in a skillet over medium heat. Remove sausage from pan, without draining it, and set aside.
2. Scramble eggs in the same pan and season with salt and pepper to taste. Remove eggs from pan and set aside.
3. Place tortillas between two damp paper towels and microwave for 20 seconds to soften.
4. Assembly-line style, add sausage, then eggs, then cheese to your tortillas. Roll, tucking the sides in as you roll.
5. You can eat the burritos just like this, wrap them in foil and freeze for later, or sear them in your sausage pan to add a little crunch to the outside. Add salsa if desired.

Yogurt Parfaits

INGREDIENTS

- 3 cups vanilla Greek yogurt
- 3/4 cup granola
- 1 cup strawberries
- 1/4 cup blueberries
- 1/4 cup raspberries
- Optional: honey

DIRECTIONS

1. Spoon Greek yogurt into four clear cups or ramekins.
2. Add granola and berries.
3. Top with honey, if using.

* PRO TIP
Granola can be packed with sugar, so look for a low-sugar option. If you're feeling fancy, add a drizzle of honey on top.

Peanut Butter Banana Toast

INGREDIENTS

- 4 slices bread (be fancy and get the bread from the bakery)
- 2 bananas
- 4 Tbsp peanut butter
- Optional: honey, cinnamon

DIRECTIONS

1. Toast bread.
2. Slice banana into thin slices.
3. Spread peanut butter onto the toast.
4. Add banana slices.

* PRO TIP
If you're feeling fancy, add a dash of cinnamon or a drizzle of honey on top!

Bagels with All the Fixin's

INGREDIENTS

- Bagels
- Optional: cream cheese (whipped is the best), Nutella, peanut butter, sliced fruit, smoked salmon

DIRECTIONS

1. Toast 'em.
2. Top 'em.
3. Eat 'em.

A few of our favorite combinations:

- Plain bagel + veggie cream cheese + sliced cucumbers
- Cinnamon raisin bagel + butter + apple butter (try the apple butter from Cracker Barrel—oh my goodness)
- Blueberry bagel + butter + strawberry jam (try the Bonne Maman jam brand and thank me later)
- Everything bagel + whipped cream cheese + smoked salmon

Monster Toast

INGREDIENTS

- Food coloring
- Milk
- Sliced white bread
- Optional: peanut butter, jelly, butter for topping

DIRECTIONS

1. In individual bowls or cups, mix your "paints" by stirring a few drops of food coloring into about 2 Tbsp of milk.
2. On plain, untoasted bread, paint a monster face using the milk-and-food coloring mixture.
3. Toast your monster-faced bread, and prepare to be amazed! Your "paint" will show up nice and bright.
4. Top with peanut butter, jelly, butter, or whatever you like.

Breakfast Banana Splits

INGREDIENTS

- 4 bananas
- 1 cup vanilla Greek yogurt
- 1 cup strawberries
- 1/4 cup granola
- 2 Tbsp peanut butter
- Optional: honey

DIRECTIONS

1. Slice bananas lengthwise and lay two slices each into four bowls.
2. Top with a few dollops of Greek yogurt.
3. Slice strawberries and sprinkle over the top. Add granola.
4. Warm peanut butter in the microwave for 15 seconds. Drizzle it over the top. Add honey if desired.

SECTION TWO

Lunch

Lunch

Buffalo Chicken Dip

"But, Emily," you say, "this is a dip, not a lunch." Oh, but I disagree! Watch me make a meal out of this deliciousness! Pair with veggie sticks or crackers. Or heck, eat it with a spoon straight from the bowl. I won't tell! (Top with a few diced green onions for a little extra color.)

 PREP TIME
15 minutes

 COOK TIME
20 minutes

 SERVINGS
6–8

perfect for a potluck

INGREDIENTS

- 8 oz cream cheese
- 1/2 cup ranch dressing
- 2 cups shredded mozzarella cheese, divided
- 2 cups shredded chicken (about 2 chicken breasts or 1 rotisserie chicken)
- 1/2 cup buffalo sauce
- Optional: 2 green onions, diced

DIRECTIONS

1. Preheat oven to 350 degrees. Spray an 8 x 8-inch baking dish with nonstick cooking spray.
2. In a saucepan over medium heat, stir together cream cheese, ranch dressing, and half the mozzarella cheese until melted and combined.
3. Add chicken and buffalo sauce and stir to combine. Pour into baking dish.
4. Top with remaining mozzarella cheese and bake for 20 minutes.

Cucumber Salad

This cucumber salad always reminds me of my mom, who makes it as a side dish. It's sweet, tangy, and crunchy. What more could you ask for? It also keeps well in the fridge for leftovers.

PREP TIME
10 minutes

COOK TIME
Refrigerate
1 hour

SERVINGS
1 to 2

INGREDIENTS

- 1/4 cup white wine vinegar
- 2 tsp sugar
- 2 cucumbers
- 1 cup grape tomatoes
- Red onion, to taste

DIRECTIONS

1. In a medium-sized bowl, mix vinegar and sugar.
2. Dice cucumbers into bite-size pieces, halve or quarter tomatoes, and slice onion into thin slices.
3. Add cucumbers and tomatoes to the dressing bowl. Add as much red onion as you'd like. Mix well. Add salt and pepper to taste.
4. Refrigerate for 1 hour before serving.

Pimento Cheese

My grandma used to make simple pimento cheese for dips and sandwiches all the time. I was unsure about it as a kid, but now that I'm older, it's a staple in our house. Pimento cheese sandwiches (on fluffy white bread, of course) are also a traditional meal at the Masters golf tournament in Augusta, Georgia. It's delicious served on good bakery bread or as a dip for veggies and crackers. Add garlic powder, onion powder, or cayenne pepper for an extra kick.

 PREP TIME
10 minutes

 COOK TIME
Refrigerate
1 hour

 SERVINGS
8

INGREDIENTS

- 6 oz cream cheese, softened
- 1/3 cup mayonnaise
- 2 cups shredded cheddar cheese
- 1 (4 oz) jar diced pimentos
- White bread or crackers, for serving

DIRECTIONS

1. In a mixing bowl, combine cream cheese, mayonnaise, cheddar cheese, and drained pimentos (reserve some of the pimento liquid). Stir to mix.
2. Stir in the liquid from the pimentos a little at a time until a smooth consistency is reached. Add salt and pepper to taste.
3. Refrigerate for 1 hour before serving on white bread or crackers.

Chicken Salad

This recipe is adapted from a beloved Pensacola restaurant long since closed: Norma's. Norma was famous for her quintessential Southern chicken salad. To date, I've never had one better. Serve the salad on its own, over lettuce, or in a croissant. This is delicious and perfect for hosting—it's my go-to for bridal or baby showers. This recipe calls for something called "chicken base." Have no fear—you'll find it in your grocery store, likely in the soup aisle, by a brand called Better Than Bouillon. It makes all the difference in the flavor of this chicken salad.

PREP TIME
20 minutes

COOK TIME
Refrigerate at least 1 hour

SERVINGS
6 to 8

INGREDIENTS

- 1 cup mayonnaise
- 2 Tbsp lemon juice
- 2 Tbsp chicken base
- 4 cups shredded (or chopped) chicken (about 3–4 chicken breasts)
- 1/2 cup diced celery
- Optional: croissants and lettuce, for serving

DIRECTIONS

1. Whisk mayonnaise, lemon juice, and chicken base together in a bowl.
2. Add chicken and celery and mix. Season with salt and pepper to taste.
3. Cover and refrigerate for 1 hour before serving. You can also refrigerate overnight and serve the next day.

 PRO TIP

If you prefer your chicken salad with more or less mayonnaise than is called for here, feel free to adjust.

Simple Arugula Salad

I had an arugula salad at a local Pensacola restaurant once. It was enormous and I ate every single bite. It was such a simple salad, but it was so delicious that I had to ask how to make the dressing. Turns out the salad is just two ingredients, and the dressing is nearly as simple! This is a staple lunch and dinner side around my house. Pair with chicken or shrimp for a boost of protein.

PREP TIME
10 minutes

COOK TIME
0 minutes

SERVINGS
4 to 6

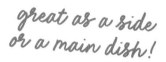

INGREDIENTS

- 1/4 cup white wine vinegar
- 1/4 cup extra virgin olive oil
- 2 Tbsp lemon juice
- 8 cups arugula
- 1/2 cup shaved Parmesan cheese
- Optional: flaky salt

DIRECTIONS

1. Combine the vinegar, olive oil, and lemon juice in a jar and shake (or whisk in a small bowl). Add salt and pepper to taste.
2. In a large salad bowl, add arugula and top with shaved Parmesan cheese.
3. Pour dressing over salad. Toss to combine.
4. Add a pinch of salt flakes to each salad if using.

Chopped Greek Salad

This salad is great for make-ahead lunches or for serving to a crowd. Add shredded chicken or chopped salami for some extra protein.

 PREP TIME
15 minutes

 COOK TIME
0 minutes

 SERVINGS
4

INGREDIENTS

- 2 cucumbers
- 1/2 red onion
- 1 cup grape tomatoes
- 1 cup pitted kalamata olives
- 1 cup crumbled feta cheese
- Greek salad dressing, to taste

DIRECTIONS

1. Chop the cucumbers, tomatoes, and red onion into bite-size pieces. Place in a medium bowl.
2. Drain the olives. Add olives and feta cheese to the bowl.
3. Toss to combine. Top with your favorite store-bought or homemade Greek salad dressing.

 PRO TIP

There are a number of wonderful premade salad dressings out there. If you have a jar and a few extra minutes, try making your own. This recipe was my grandmother's go-to and I can promise you, it will not disappoint: simply combine equal parts vegetable oil, white vinegar, and sugar (or sugar substitute). I like to add a little salt and pepper to my salad, but you can also add those straight into the dressing.

Tuna Salad

I'm a big tuna fan. When I was a kid, a tuna sandwich on white bread was my idea of a perfect lunch. These days, I skip the bread and make this protein-packed, fiber-forward salad. Use a vegetable chopper to get your veggies nice and small for the perfect bite. These salads are also a great way to use up any leftover or extra veggies you have lying around! Just about anything is delicious in this salad.

 PREP TIME
10 minutes

 COOK TIME
0 minutes

 SERVINGS
2

INGREDIENTS

- 2 stalks celery
- 1 green bell pepper
- 1/2 red onion
- 2 (5 oz) cans tuna, drained
- 1/4 cup mayonnaise
- Optional: lettuce, greens, or bread for serving

DIRECTIONS

1. Chop celery, bell pepper, and red onion into small, similar-sized pieces. I chop the veggies very small (or use the tiny side of the veggie chopper) so they give just the right amount of crunch.
2. Add veggies to a bowl with the drained tuna. Add mayonnaise, then salt and black pepper to taste. Stir to combine.
3. Serve in lettuce cups, on top of a bed of greens, on a sandwich, or simply enjoy it with a fork.

Simple Cobb Salad

I absolutely love a Cobb salad. It's filling and full of protein and nutrients. Most of the time, I let my kids assemble their own so they can add the toppings they like best. This is a great way to easily feed a group where each person has different tastes and preferences.

 PREP TIME
20 minutes

 COOK TIME
20–30 minutes

 SERVINGS
4 to 6

INGREDIENTS

- 4 strips bacon
- 1 bag pre-chopped romaine lettuce
- 2 cups chopped rotisserie chicken (or 2 breasts, baked and chopped)
- 1 (15 oz) can corn
- 1 cup cherry tomatoes
- 1/2 cup crumbled blue cheese or feta cheese
- Honey mustard or ranch dressing, for serving

DIRECTIONS

1. Bake bacon on a sheet pan at 400 degrees for 20 to 30 minutes.
2. While bacon is cooking, add lettuce to a salad bowl or large tray.
3. Add chicken, corn, tomatoes, and cheese in strips across the top of the lettuce.
4. When bacon is finished baking, place on a paper towel to drain. Roughly chop, then add as another strip on top of the salad.
5. Serve with honey mustard or ranch dressing.

 PRO TIP

For a heartier salad and more topping options, add avocado, red onions, or hard-boiled eggs cut in half. Cobb salad is great with store-bought ranch or honey mustard dressing. If you're feeling adventurous and want to make your own, try this: Add 1/4 cup red wine vinegar, 1/2 cup extra virgin olive oil, and 1 tsp Dijon mustard to a jar. Shake to combine. Voilà!

Caprese Salad

This salad is a crowd favorite, more than likely because it doesn't contain lettuce! If you're feeling fancy, you can also assemble these ingredients on toothpicks for little finger food–style salad bites!

PREP TIME
10 minutes

COOK TIME
0 minutes

SERVINGS
4 to 6

INGREDIENTS

- 1 1/2 cups grape tomatoes
- 1/2 cup fresh basil leaves
- 8 oz mozzarella cheese pearls
- 2 Tbsp olive oil
- 1 Tbsp balsamic glaze (balsamic vinegar will work in a pinch!)
- Optional: sliced red onion

DIRECTIONS

1. Halve the grape tomatoes.
2. Roughly chop the basil leaves.
3. Add the tomatoes, basil, and mozzarella cheese to a medium bowl.
4. Drizzle the olive oil and balsamic glaze over top (do not stir, or your entire salad will turn the color of the balsamic).
5. Season with salt and pepper to taste.

✳ PRO TIP

Balsamic glaze is also known as a balsamic reduction. Additional sweeteners like honey or sugar might be added. You can make this yourself by simmering balsamic vinegar in a saucepan until it has reduced and thickened to a maple syrup consistency, or you can buy it premade in the vinegar section at the store.

Tomato Soup

It doesn't get much simpler or yummier than this recipe. Don't forget to top the soup with Goldfish crackers. This recipe is made with an immersion blender (although you can use a regular blender if you don't mind washing the extra dishes). Don't be intimidated by the immersion blender. Once you've tried it, you'll find a bunch of ways you can put it to good use in your kitchen. For the canned tomatoes, we like San Marzano.

PREP TIME
10 minutes

COOK TIME
40 minutes

SERVINGS
4

INGREDIENTS

- 1/2 yellow onion
- 1/4 cup (1/2 stick) butter
- 1 (28 oz) can whole peeled tomatoes, with juices
- 1 1/2 cups vegetable broth
- Goldfish crackers, for topping

DIRECTIONS

1. Cut onion into wedges.
2. In a medium pot over medium heat, melt butter.
3. Add the onion, tomatoes, and broth. Bring to a simmer.
4. Cook on medium-low, uncovered, for about 30 minutes.
5. Add salt to taste.
6. Using an immersion blender, blend soup to desired consistency (either fully smooth or with a little texture from the tomatoes—both ways are great).
7. Spoon into bowls and top with Goldfish crackers.

ell

Ramen Noodle Bowls

I *love* ramen noodles. I never did the whole college ramen noodle thing, but I love a warm bowl as a comfort meal every now and then. This meal is super simple, filling, and totally customizable to fit your family's tastes.

PREP TIME
10 minutes

COOK TIME
10 minutes

SERVINGS
4

INGREDIENTS

- 8 cups chicken broth
- 1/4 cup soy sauce
- 4 (3 oz) packages chicken-flavored ramen noodles
- 1 (12 oz) bag frozen mixed vegetables
- 1 tsp sesame oil
- Optional: cooked ground chicken, sliced green onions, sesame seeds, chili garlic sauce

DIRECTIONS

1. In a saucepan, heat chicken broth and soy sauce.
2. Add ramen noodles and frozen vegetables to broth, breaking noodles apart as they cook.
3. Cook noodles according to the ramen package directions. Cook veggies.
4. Once noodles are soft, sprinkle the seasoning packet and sesame oil over top. Stir well.

 PRO TIP

If you're feeling fancy, add cooked ground chicken to the noodles for some extra protein; top with sliced green onions and sesame seeds. A little chili garlic sauce also tastes great drizzled on top.

Ramen Chicken Salad

We ate this salad a lot growing up, so it's pretty nostalgic for me. You will eat every bite because each bite is the perfect mix of sweet, savory, and crunchy. My mom almost always served this salad with blueberry muffins (boxed muffins are great) and fruit salad.

PREP TIME
15 minutes

COOK TIME
5 minutes

SERVINGS
4 to 6

INGREDIENTS

For the Dressing
- 1/2 cup canola oil
- 1/2 cup white vinegar
- 1/2 cup sugar
- 1 seasoning packet from ramen noodles

For the Salad
- 4 boneless, skinless chicken breasts
- 1 bag pre-chopped romaine lettuce
- 1 (14 oz) bag coleslaw
- 1/4 cup sliced almonds
- 2 (3 oz) packages ramen noodles, chicken flavored

DIRECTIONS

1. In a small bowl, whisk together all dressing ingredients. Refrigerate until ready to use.
2. Place 4 chicken breasts in a large pot. Cover chicken with water and bring to a boil. Once boiling, reduce heat to low, cover, and simmer for 15–20 minutes or until chicken is fully cooked (internal temperature should reach 165°F). Remove chicken from the pot and let it cool.
3. Add the chicken, coleslaw, and lettuce to a large bowl.
4. In a medium, dry pan, warm the almonds and ramen noodles over medium heat until toasted (break the noodles up as you add them to the pan), being careful not to burn.
5. Let almonds and noodles cool, then add to the lettuce, coleslaw, and chicken. Pour the dressing over the salad. Toss to combine, then serve.

Lunch
Assembly Meals

| assembly meal: | a quick, easy dish made by combining ready-to-use ingredients with little or no cooking. see also: lifesaver. |

Hawaiian Roll Sandwiches

INGREDIENTS

- 12 Hawaiian sweet rolls
- 1 lb sliced deli ham
- 1/2 lb sliced white American cheese

DIRECTIONS

1. Slice the whole pack of Hawaiian rolls horizontally, separating the tops from the bottoms.
2. Arrange ham then cheese on the bottom halves. Replace top of the roll pack.
3. Use a knife to cut individual sandwiches apart.
4. Enjoy! Or place in baggies and freeze for future lunches.

Chicken Caesar Wraps

INGREDIENTS

- 1 rotisserie chicken
- 1 bag pre-chopped romaine lettuce
- 1/3 cup grated Parmesan cheese
- 8 to 10 tortillas
- Caesar dressing, to taste

DIRECTIONS

1. Pull rotisserie chicken meat from bone and shred it.
2. Assemble! Add lettuce, chicken, and Parmesan cheese to your tortilla, then top with Caesar dressing, roll, and slice.

Ham & Cheese Rollups

INGREDIENTS

- 4 spreadable soft cheese wedges (Laughing Cow is our favorite)
- 4 tortillas
- 8 slices deli ham
- 1 cup baby spinach
- Chips or fresh veggies, for serving

DIRECTIONS

1. Spread cheese across each entire tortilla.
2. Cover tortillas with deli ham slices.
3. Top with baby spinach.
4. Roll tightly and slice into pinwheels.
5. Serve with chips or fresh veggies.

Protein Snack Plate

INGREDIENTS

These ingredients depend on what I have on hand. I try to check each box below.

- **Protein:** leftover grilled chicken, a meat stick, a boiled egg, deli meat rollup
- **Healthy fat:** sliced avocado, hummus, cheese, olives, nut butter, nuts
- **Fiber:** fruit, celery, carrot sticks

DIRECTIONS

1. The key to a protein snack plate is to make sure you include enough protein to constitute a full meal. Get creative with what you have on hand! I use leftovers when possible but sometimes keep things like Chomps beef jerky on hand to grab in a pinch.
2. Assemble items on a plate rather than snacking from the containers. C'mon now. Then enjoy!

Simple Pasta Salad

INGREDIENTS

- 1 (16 oz) box bowtie pasta
- 1 cup Italian dressing (we love Olive Garden)
- 1/2 cup grated Parmesan cheese
- 1/4 cup sliced green olives

DIRECTIONS

1. Boil pasta according to the directions on the package until al dente, about 7 minutes.
2. Drain pasta and rinse with cold water. Place in a medium bowl.
3. Add dressing, Parmesan cheese, and green olives. Stir to combine.
4. Refrigerate for 1 to 2 hours before serving.

The Superior Grilled Cheese

INGREDIENTS

- 3 slices white bread
- 1 Tbsp mayonnaise
- 2 to 4 slices of American cheese (we like Kraft)

* double decker

DIRECTIONS

1. Spread a thin layer of mayonnaise on one side each of three slices of bread.
2. Warm a skillet over medium heat.
3. Place one slice of bread in the skillet, mayonnaise side down, then top with two cheese slices. Top the cheese with another slice of bread, mayonnaise side up.
4. Toast for about three minutes (until golden brown), then flip to toast the other side. Once that side is toasted, top with more cheese and the last piece of bread, mayonnaise side up. Now you have a double-decker sandwich (bread, cheese, bread, cheese, bread).
5. Flip the sandwich so the newest piece of bread is now on the bottom, mayonnaise side down. Toast for three minutes or until golden brown.

Cottage Cheese Bowls

INGREDIENTS

- 1 red bell pepper
- 1 yellow bell pepper
- 1 cucumber
- 1 cup cottage cheese
- 8 to 10 pitted kalamata olives

DIRECTIONS

1. Chop veggies using your vegetable chopper or a knife— whatever floats your boat. Try to keep the veggies the same size-ish. Or don't. It literally doesn't matter. It's going to taste delicious no matter what.
2. Place cottage cheese in a medium bowl, add chopped veggies and olives, and mix well.
3. Add salt and pepper to taste.

Dorito Sandwiches

INGREDIENTS

- 8 slices white bread
- 4 slices white American cheese
- 8 slices deli ham
- Mustard to taste
- Doritos, preferably from the red bag, but any kind will do

My kids remember this as our "pandemic" lockdown lunch!

DIRECTIONS

1. Lay all 8 pieces of bread on a greased or lined baking sheet. Top 4 with cheese.
2. Add ham on the other 4 pieces of bread (so both the cheese and ham get toasty).
3. At this point, you can broil them. But if you turn on that broiler, you'd better not walk away. Crack the oven and watch it the entire time. The bread will burn very quickly if left unattended, and it could even catch fire. Moral of the story: don't mess with the broiler. If you choose to avoid the broiler—like me—just bake the sandwiches at 350 degrees. Check them every couple of minutes until you like how toasty they look.
4. Remove baking sheet from oven, top ham with mustard and Doritos, and then put the sandwiches together.
5. Use the palm of your hand to smash your sandwiches, then cut diagonally. This step is a must.

Turkey, Apple & Cheddar Sandwiches

INGREDIENTS

- 8 slices whole wheat bread
- 1 Honeycrisp apple
- 8 slices deli turkey
- 4 slices cheddar cheese
- Optional: mayonnaise

DIRECTIONS

1. If you're feeling fancy, toast the bread first. The sandwich is equally good untoasted.
2. Slice apple into thin slices.
3. Assemble sandwiches by topping 4 bread slices with turkey, cheese, apple slices, and then the other slices of bread. If you're a mayonnaise fan, add a thin layer to the bread before assembly.

Easy Chicken Wraps

INGREDIENTS

- 1 (11.5 oz) salad kit (we like Taylor Farms)
- 2 cups shredded chicken (about 2 chicken breasts or 1 rotisserie chicken)
- 4 tortillas

DIRECTIONS

1. Open salad kit and remove dressing and toppings packets.
2. Lay out tortillas and spread the salad on top in a line.
3. Place a mound of shredded chicken on top of lettuce.
4. Sprinkle any toppings from salad kit on top of chicken.
5. Add dressing as a sauce for the wrap.
6. Roll gently, tucking ends in like a burrito as you go.
7. Slice at an angle and enjoy!

Pizza Rollups

INGREDIENTS

- 8 flour tortillas
- 3/4 cup pizza sauce
- 1/2 to 1 cup pepperoni slices
- 8 string cheese sticks
- 2 Tbsp olive oil

DIRECTIONS

1. Spray an air fryer basket with nonstick cooking spray, or line it with parchment paper liner. Preheat to 375 degrees.
2. Soften tortillas by wrapping them with a damp paper towel and microwaving them for about 30 seconds.
3. Lay tortillas flat and spoon a bit of pizza sauce onto each. Lay a few pepperoni slices on top of sauce.
4. Split string cheese in half lengthwise. Lay each half on top of pepperoni.
5. Roll up tortillas, brush with olive oil (for crispiness), and place seam side down in air fryer.
6. Air fry for about 5 minutes.

Spinach & Strawberry Salad

INGREDIENTS

- 8 cups baby spinach
- 1 1/2 cups strawberries
- 3/4 cup pecan pieces
- 3/4 cup crumbled feta cheese
- 1/2 cup raspberry walnut vinaigrette dressing (we like Paul Newman's)

DIRECTIONS

1. Slice strawberries and lightly toast pecan pieces.
2. Place the baby spinach, strawberries, pecans, and feta cheese in a medium salad bowl.
3. Top with the dressing and toss. Serve immediately.

SECTION THREE

Dinner

Dinner

RECIPES

ASSEMBLY MEALS

Baked Feta Pasta

A version of this recipe—created by Finnish blogger Jenni Häyrinen (@liemessa)—went viral on TikTok. And for good reason! It's so easy to make and is absolutely delicious. Serve with warm French bread and a side salad if you're feeling fancy.

 PREP TIME
10 minutes

 COOK TIME
30 minutes

 SERVINGS
8 to 12

INGREDIENTS

- 1 (8 oz) block feta cheese
- 2 cups cherry tomatoes
- 3 Tbsp olive oil
- 1 (16 oz) box bowtie pasta
- 1/4 cup chopped basil, for topping

DIRECTIONS

1. Preheat oven to 400 degrees. Spray a 9 x 13-inch baking dish with nonstick cooking spray.
2. Place feta cheese in center of baking dish, and place the tomatoes around the feta.
3. Drizzle olive oil over entire dish, then add salt and black pepper to taste.
4. Bake for 30 minutes, then remove and stir.
5. While feta and tomatoes are baking, boil bowtie pasta according to instructions on the package until al dente. Drain pasta and add to the baking dish, stirring thoroughly to combine.
6. Top with chopped basil.

 PRO TIP

Reserve one cup of pasta water in case your feta tomato sauce is too thick to coat all the pasta. Add a little at a time to thin it out.

Chicken & Rice Casserole

If my kids have a favorite weeknight dinner, this is it. I'm not entirely sure why, but we serve it with canned cranberry sauce. It's tradition. This makes great leftovers the next day as well. If your kids don't like mushrooms, don't worry. You can hardly taste or see them in the finished dish.

 PREP TIME
15 minutes

 COOK TIME
1 hour

 SERVINGS
6 to 8

INGREDIENTS

- 4 boneless skinless chicken breasts
- 2 cups chicken broth
- 1 (10.5 oz) can condensed cream of mushroom soup
- 1 (10.5 oz) can condensed cream of chicken soup
- 1 (10.5 oz) can condensed cream of celery soup
- 2 cups uncooked instant rice
- 1/2 cup (1 stick) butter, sliced into 10 to 12 pieces

DIRECTIONS

1. Preheat oven to 400 degrees. Spray a 9 x 13-inch baking dish with nonstick cooking spray.
2. Cut chicken breasts into cubes.
3. Mix chicken broth, condensed soups, and rice in a large bowl. Add cubed chicken.
4. Pour mixture into baking dish.
5. Place butter slices evenly across top of the mixture.
6. Cover and bake for 60 minutes, until chicken reaches internal temperature of 165 degrees. Cool for 15 minutes before serving.

White Chicken Enchiladas

This recipe comes from an old family friend who shared it with me as her go-to many years ago. It's become my favorite dish to double and both feed my family and deliver to a new mom or friend going through a hard time. Bonus: these freeze wonderfully and are a great make-ahead meal.

 PREP TIME
10 minutes

 COOK TIME
30 minutes

 SERVINGS
4 to 6

my favorite dish to take to a new mom

INGREDIENTS

- 2 cups shredded chicken (about 2 breasts or 1 rotisserie chicken)
- 1/2 cup milk
- 1/2 cup salsa verde
- 1 (10.5 oz) can cream of chicken soup
- 1 cup shredded Mexican-style cheese, divided
- 2 Tbsp chopped cilantro, divided
- 10 flour tortillas

DIRECTIONS

1. Preheat oven to 350 degrees. Spray a 9 x 13-inch baking dish with nonstick cooking spray.
2. To a mixing bowl, add chicken, milk, salsa verde, cream of chicken soup, half the cheese, and half the cilantro. Stir to combine.
3. Divide mixture in half.
4. Fill tortillas with half the chicken mixture. Roll to close. Line them up in the pan seam side down.
5. Pour remaining chicken mixture over enchiladas, and top with remaining cheese and cilantro.
6. Cover with foil and bake for 30 minutes.

✳ PRO TIP

You can make several substitutions to this recipe if you'd like to lighten it up. Swap in wheat tortillas for more fiber. And choose a low-fat cheese for fewer overall calories.

Air-Fried Salmon Bites

Everything tastes better when cooked in the air fryer. These salmon bites are crunchy and packed with protein. If you're introducing salmon to your child for the first time, this is a great way to do it. Serve it as your main dish or in a bowl over rice.

 PREP TIME
10 minutes

 COOK TIME
15 minutes

 SERVINGS
3 to 4

INGREDIENTS

- 2 fresh salmon filets
- 1/2 cup brown sugar
- 2 Tbsp olive oil
- Zest from 1/2 lemon
- Juice from 1/2 lemon

DIRECTIONS

1. Preheat air fryer to 400 degrees. Spray with nonstick cooking spray or use an air fryer liner.
2. If needed, remove salmon skin and pat dry.
3. Slice the salmon into bite-size nuggets.
4. In a large bowl, combine brown sugar, olive oil, lemon zest, and lemon juice.
5. Add salmon to the bowl and gently toss to coat each piece.
6. Air fry salmon bites for 8 minutes. Flip the salmon bites and air fry for another 5 minutes.

Egg Roll Bowls

I'm hungry just thinking about this bowl. It's super easy to make, kid and picky husband approved, and packed with fiber and protein. I make this a few times a month and save the leftovers for lunch.

 PREP TIME
10 minutes

 COOK TIME
10 minutes

 SERVINGS
4

INGREDIENTS

- 1 lb ground pork
- 2 (14 oz) bags coleslaw
- 3 Tbsp soy sauce
- 1 tsp sesame oil
- 2 garlic cloves, minced

DIRECTIONS

1. Brown ground pork over medium heat. Add coleslaw and cook mixture until slaw is partially cooked down and soft, about 3 minutes.
2. In a small mixing bowl, stir together soy sauce, sesame oil, and garlic. Pour into the skillet.
3. Continue to cook about 3 minutes, until coleslaw is fully cooked down.

 PRO TIP

If you're feeling fancy, top the dish with sliced green onions (just the green part), shelled edamame, or sesame seeds. You could even mix in a little brown rice or serve the rice alongside your egg roll bowls.

Sheet Pan Chicken Fajitas

I read somewhere once that ordering fajitas at a restaurant is the ultimate flex. The steaming hot cast-iron plate draws the attention of the whole place when it's served. This recipe has less fanfare but is equally delicious. Serve on its own or with tortillas, and use different colors of bell peppers.

 PREP TIME
15 minutes

 COOK TIME
25 minutes

 SERVINGS
4 to 6

INGREDIENTS

- 4 boneless skinless chicken breasts
- 3 bell peppers
- 1 red onion
- 2 Tbsp olive oil
- 1 (1 oz) fajita seasoning packet
- 8 flour tortillas

DIRECTIONS

1. Preheat oven to 400 degrees.
2. Slice chicken, peppers, and onion into strips.
3. Put strips in a gallon-size plastic bag. Add olive oil and fajita seasoning. Shake bag to fully coat each strip.
4. Arrange seasoned ingredients on a baking sheet in a single layer.
5. Bake for 20 to 25 minutes. If you like your chicken a little extra brown, turn the broiler on at the end (just keep an eye on it so nothing burns).
6. Warm tortillas by placing a stack of them in the microwave wrapped in a wet paper towel for 30 seconds. Serve fajitas with warm tortillas.

✳ PRO TIP

Serve with any toppings you love and have on hand: shredded cheese, queso fresco, salsa, sour cream, lime wedges, guacamole, or cilantro. For an extra kick, squeeze a lime into the plastic bag of chicken before shaking.

Coca-Cola Pot Roast

I swear my mom shared this recipe with me, but she also swears she doesn't put Coca Cola in her pot roast. I, however, do! And I think if you try this, it'll become your go-to pot roast recipe. It's so easy that I can throw it together while making lunches on a busy school morning.

 **PREP TIME**
10 minutes

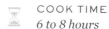 **COOK TIME**
6 to 8 hours

 **SERVINGS**
4 to 6

so good at the end of a busy day

INGREDIENTS

- 3 to 4-lb chuck roast
- 1 yellow onion
- 1 (16 oz) bag baby carrots
- 1 lb small potatoes
- 1 (12 oz) can Coca-Cola
- 1 (2 oz) packet onion soup mix

DIRECTIONS

1. Spray your slow cooker with nonstick cooking spray or use a liner (you'll thank me when it's time to clean the slow cooker).
2. Quarter onion and halve potatoes.
3. Put chuck roast, onion, carrots, and potatoes in slow cooker. Add Coca-Cola and onion soup mix.
4. Cover and cook on low for 6 to 8 hours.

Meatloaf Cupcakes

"Ma! The meatloaf?!" Anybody? Okay, that was a reference to Will Ferrell's character in *Wedding Crashers* (you must watch it). Everyone loves meatloaf, but meatloaf "cupcakes" are next-level fun. These freeze great too!

 PREP TIME
10 minutes

 COOK TIME
35 minutes

 SERVINGS
6

INGREDIENTS

- 2 lbs ground beef
- 1 (6 oz) box stuffing mix (such as Stove Top)
- 2 eggs
- 1/2 cup ketchup
- 1/2 cup water
- Optional: 1 (24 oz) container refrigerated mashed potatoes, 12 green peas

DIRECTIONS

1. Preheat oven to 350 degrees. Spray a 12-muffin pan with nonstick cooking spray.
2. In a large bowl, combine ground beef, stuffing mix, eggs, ketchup, and water, and mix well by hand.
3. Fill muffin cups 3/4 full of meatloaf mixture.
4. Bake for 35 minutes.

✳ PRO TIP

To turn these muffins into cupcakes, make mashed potatoes (or, if you're me, warm up a pan of Bob Evans premade mashed potatoes), and put them in a plastic bag. Snip one corner to use it as a piping bag. Pretend those potatoes are icing and ice your "muffins." If you're feeling extra fancy, place one pea on top of each muffin. Your kids will get a big giggle. If you'd like to serve these with a dipping sauce, combine equal parts ketchup and brown sugar.

Tater Tot Casserole

If you're looking for a super-healthy meal for those days when you're trying to keep it light, well, keep looking. But if you're looking for a slam-dunk comfort-food meal, look no further. This is pure happiness in a 9 x 13-inch baking dish.

PREP TIME
10 minutes

COOK TIME
40 minutes

SERVINGS
8 to 12

my most requested slumber party dinner!

INGREDIENTS

- 1 lb ground beef
- 1 (10.5 oz) can cream of celery soup
- 1 (32 oz) bag frozen tater tots
- 1 cup shredded cheddar cheese
- Optional: 4 green onions, diced

DIRECTIONS

1. Preheat oven to 350 degrees. Spray a 9 x 13-inch baking dish with nonstick cooking spray.
2. Brown ground beef over medium heat. Drain the excess fat and discard. Stir in cream of celery soup.
3. Spread mixture into the baking dish.
4. Top mixture with a single layer of frozen tater tots. You won't need the whole bag.
5. Sprinkle cheese evenly over tater tots.
6. Bake for 40 minutes.
7. Remove from oven and top with sliced green onions.

DINNER

Classic Chicken Soup

My friend Gina taught me how to make this chicken soup when she was visiting once from chilly Minnesota. Since then, it's my go-to when someone's sick or when it's extra brisk outside.

PREP TIME
10 minutes

COOK TIME
30 minutes

SERVINGS
4 to 6

INGREDIENTS

- 4 carrots
- 4 celery stalks
- 1 yellow onion
- 1/4 cup (1/2 stick) butter
- 1 rotisserie chicken, shredded*
- 4 cups chicken broth, plus more as needed

DIRECTIONS

1. Dice carrots, celery, and onion.
2. In a large soup pot, warm butter until it is mostly melted. Add vegetables and sauté until tender.
3. Add shredded rotisserie chicken and chicken broth. If you'd like more liquid, you can add additional broth or water to the pot. Season with salt and pepper to taste.
4. Bring soup to a boil, then cover and simmer for 30 minutes.

* If you don't want to use a rotisserie chicken, you can boil 3 chicken breasts until they reach 165 degrees internally, then shred them with two forks or a hand mixer.

 PRO TIP

For chicken noodle soup, you can increase the chicken broth to 8 cups and add one-third of a box of pasta to the soup halfway through simmering. For extra flavor, add 1/2 tsp turmeric.

Game Day Chili

Football is a big deal at our house. I may not totally understand what's happening on the television, but I do know I'm going to be making something delicious in the kitchen. This chili recipe is intended for a slow cooker, but you can also make it on the stove if you don't have enough slow-cooking time.

PREP TIME
10 minutes

COOK TIME
6 to 8 hours

SERVINGS
4 to 6

INGREDIENTS

- 1 lb ground beef
- 1 yellow onion
- 1 (16 oz) can beans (whatever type you like: we love black beans and kidney beans)
- 2 (14.5 oz) cans diced tomatoes with green chilies*
- 2 Tbsp chili powder

DIRECTIONS

1. Spray a slow cooker with nonstick cooking spray.
2. Brown ground beef over medium heat. Drain the excess fat and discard, and add beef to slow cooker.
3. Chop onion and add it to slow cooker.
4. Drain and rinse beans. Add them to the slow cooker.
5. Add tomatoes with chilies and chili powder and stir.
6. Cover and cook on high for 4 to 6 hours or on low for 6 to 8 hours.
7. Top with your favorite chili toppings.

*If you like a little extra spice, swap the tomatoes for 2 cans of fire-roasted diced tomatoes with green chilies.

 PRO TIP

Let everyone dress up their chili the way they like. Serve the chili with topping options like shredded cheese, sour cream, avocado slices, pickled jalapeños, cilantro, tortilla chips, and lime wedges.

Super Simple Pasta

This recipe will always make me think of chilly nights at a cabin in the Blue Ridge Mountains. Reminiscent of Hamburger Helper, this hearty dish is always a favorite meal for little kids, teenagers, and adults alike.

 PREP TIME
0 minutes

 COOK TIME
20 minutes

 SERVINGS
4 to 6

INGREDIENTS

- 1 lb ground beef
- 2 cups beef broth
- 2 cups milk
- 1 Tbsp ketchup
- 1 (16 oz) box elbow macaroni
- 1 cup shredded cheddar cheese

DIRECTIONS

1. Brown ground beef in a large skillet or Dutch oven. Drain fat and discard it.
2. Add beef broth, milk, ketchup, and salt and pepper to taste, then bring to a boil.
3. Add macaroni, then simmer uncovered, for 10–12 minutes or until liquid is mostly absorbed.
4. Add cheese and stir everything together.
5. Serve and enjoy!

Spaghetti Squash & Meat Sauce

Save your arm muscles and prep your spaghetti squash for cutting by softening it in the microwave: poke the sides with a fork, pop it in the microwave for 5 minutes, and the squash will be nice and tender, ready for the knife. This recipe is savory, healthy-ish, and loved by all.

 PREP TIME
10 minutes

 COOK TIME
*1 hour and
15 minutes*

 SERVINGS
4

INGREDIENTS

- 2 spaghetti squash
- 1 yellow onion
- 1 lb ground beef
- 1 (24 oz) jar marinara sauce
- 2 1/2 cups mozzarella cheese, divided
- Optional: grated Parmesan cheese and flat-leaf parsley to top

DIRECTIONS

1. Preheat oven to 375 degrees. Spray two 9 x 13-inch baking dishes with nonstick cooking spray.
2. Soften squash in the microwave. Slice each squash lengthwise. Scoop out the seeds and discard. Place squash halves, cut sides down, in baking dishes. Roast for 45 minutes.
3. While spaghetti squash is roasting, dice onion.
4. Brown ground beef in a skillet. Drain the excess fat and discard. Add diced onion and sauté until tender.
5. Add marinara sauce, stir, and set heat to simmer while you finish the rest of the steps.
6. Using a fork, rake over the inside of squash halves to make strands and place them in a medium-size bowl. Set empty shells back on baking dishes.
7. Add 1 cup cheese to the bowl of spaghetti squash strands and stir to combine. Spoon 1/4 of squash mixture into each empty shell. Then divide meat sauce among the squash halves.
8. Top with remaining cheese and bake for 25 minutes.
9. Garnish with grated Parmesan and parsley if desired.

Foil Packet Dinner

Years ago, when my kids were tiny, my best friend, Kristin, and her husband used to come over for Sunday night suppers at our house. One time she made foil packet meals, and I was hooked: they're so easy and delicious.

 PREP TIME
10 minutes

 COOK TIME
45 minutes

 SERVINGS
4

INGREDIENTS

- 1 lb ground beef
- 1 (1 oz) packet onion soup mix
- 1 lb small potatoes
- 2 (14.5 oz) cans green beans
- 4 Tbsp butter, divided
- Optional: finely chopped parsley to top

DIRECTIONS

1. Preheat oven to 400 degrees.
2. Cut 4 pieces of aluminum foil, 18-ish inches long each, and spray them with nonstick cooking spray.
3. Using your hands, mix ground beef and onion soup mix in a bowl. Divide the mixture into 4 and roll them into balls. Smash the tops of the balls slightly to make them flatter, but not as flat as a hamburger patty.
4. Wash and quarter potatoes. Place one-quarter of the potatoes in the center of each piece of aluminum foil.
5. Drain green beans and place an even portion on top of the potatoes in each packet.
6. Place beef patties on top of vegetables.
7. Place 1 Tbsp of butter on top of each beef patty.
8. Close each aluminum foil packet by pulling up the sides then bringing the other two sides to meet.
9. Bake for 45 minutes, or until patties reach 160 degrees internally.

Easy Shrimp Boil

We love a good shrimp boil at our house. We even had one at our wedding reception! This simple sheet pan shrimp boil will blow you away.

PREP TIME
10 minutes

COOK TIME
30 minutes

SERVINGS
4 to 6

INGREDIENTS

- 1 lb small yellow potatoes
- 3 ears corn
- 1/4 cup (1/2 stick) butter
- 1 lb raw shrimp (I like peeled and deveined)
- 1 Tbsp Old Bay seasoning
- Optional: andouille sausage and onion, parsley, and lemon wedges to garnish

DIRECTIONS

1. Preheat oven to 400 degrees. Line a baking sheet with parchment paper.
2. Bring a large pot of water to a boil. Once boiling, add potatoes and cook until tender, about 12 minutes.
3. Cut ears of corn into smaller pieces and boil with potatoes during the last 5 minutes, then drain.
4. Melt butter in a bowl in the microwave. Combine butter with Old Bay seasoning.
5. Place shrimp, potatoes, and corn on the baking sheet.
6. Pour butter mixture over everything.
7. Bake for 15 minutes, or until shrimp are pink and opaque.

 PRO TIP

You can also easily throw in some andouille sausage and yellow onion. Thinly slice the sausage and onions, and add them to the baking sheet before the butter mixture. If you're feeling fancy, garnish with fresh minced parsley, and serve with garlic bread and lemon wedges.

Easy Edamame Stir-Fry

Do you ever find your body craving vegetables? I do! My favorite way to honor this craving is with a big bowl of this edamame stir-fry. Eat it as a vegetarian dish or add rotisserie chicken, skirt steak, or even ground pork for extra protein.

 PREP TIME
10 minutes

 COOK TIME
10 minutes

 SERVINGS
4

INGREDIENTS

- 2 Tbsp olive oil
- 1 (14 oz) bag coleslaw
- 1 (12 oz) bag frozen shelled edamame
- 1 (8 to 10 oz) bag steam-in-bag rice
- 2 Tbsp soy sauce

DIRECTIONS

1. Warm a saucepan over medium heat, then add olive oil to the warm pan.
2. Add coleslaw mix to the pan. Sauté over medium heat until coleslaw's volume is reduced, about 4 to 6 minutes.
3. Add shelled edamame to the pan and continue to sauté.
4. While the stir-fry cooks, heat brown rice in the microwave according to the instructions on package.
5. Add rice and soy sauce to pan.
6. Continue to stir until all the flavors come together. Remove from heat and serve.

Chicken Pot Pie Casserole

What's better than chicken pot pie? Chicken pot pie when you don't have to mess with a piecrust! *This* recipe uses canned biscuit dough and is super easy to make. For the biscuits, we like Pillsbury Grands.

PREP TIME
10 minutes

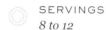

COOK TIME
35 minutes

SERVINGS
8 to 12

INGREDIENTS

- 2 cups shredded, cooked chicken (about 2 chicken breasts or 1 rotisserie chicken)
- 1 (12 oz) bag frozen mixed vegetables
- 1 (10.5 oz) can cream of chicken soup
- 1 cup chicken broth
- 1 (16.3 oz) can biscuits

DIRECTIONS

1. Preheat oven to 375 degrees. Spray a 9 x 13-inch baking dish with nonstick cooking spray.
2. In a large pot over medium-low heat, warm chicken, vegetables, and both cans of soup. Add salt and pepper to taste.
3. Smooth chicken mixture into baking dish.
4. Arrange biscuits on top of chicken mixture.
5. Bake for 20 to 25 minutes, until top is golden brown.
6. Serve while hot.

Perfect Baked Chicken Breasts

I use leftovers from this recipe in side dishes, or I pair them with a good salad. And some nights, I just dip the leftover chicken in honey mustard and call it a day.

 PREP TIME
10 minutes

 COOK TIME
20 minutes

 SERVINGS
4

INGREDIENTS

- 1/2 tsp paprika
- 1/2 tsp garlic powder
- 1 tsp salt
- 1/2 tsp pepper
- 4 boneless skinless chicken breasts
- 1/4 cup (1/2 stick) butter, melted

DIRECTIONS

1. Preheat oven to 425 degrees.
2. Mix paprika, garlic powder, salt, and pepper in a small bowl.
3. Pound chicken breasts with a meat mallet or heavy skillet. You want them to be about 1/4 to 1/2 inch thick. This is a pain, I know. You don't have to do it. But having them all the same thickness helps the chicken cook evenly.
4. Lay chicken in a baking dish, and brush both sides of the chicken breasts with the melted butter. Sprinkle the seasoning mixture all over both sides of chicken breasts.
5. Bake for 18 to 20 minutes, or until the internal temperature of the chicken is 165 degrees.
6. Let the chicken rest for 5 minutes before serving.

Taco Turkey Skillet

My mom made this for our family once and it was an absolute home run. Plus, it got my family to eat zucchini! They didn't even realize it. In fact, they started second-guessing their staunch stance against the vegetable when they discovered the actual ingredients. What a win.

 PREP TIME
10 minutes

 COOK TIME
15 minutes

 SERVINGS
4 to 6

INGREDIENTS

- 1 lb ground turkey
- 2 zucchini
- 1 (1 oz) packet taco seasoning
- 1 (15 oz) can black beans
- 1 cup shredded cheddar cheese

DIRECTIONS

1. Brown ground turkey in a skillet over medium heat until it is cooked through.
2. Chop zucchini and add it to the pan.
3. Add taco seasoning and stir.
4. Drain and rinse black beans. Add them to the pan.
5. Cook on low to allow flavors to combine, 3 to 4 minutes. Then top with shredded cheese. Remove from heat.
6. Serve with your favorite taco-type toppings.

✳ PRO TIP

Set out a variety of taco toppings for your family to make their own taco bowls: sour cream, salsa, shredded lettuce, chopped tomatoes, avocados, and tortilla chips will work great.

Slow Cooker Turkey Meatballs

My family absolutely loves meatballs. These turkey meatballs are light, easy, and fun to make. Pair them with a vegetable side (broccoli and cheese is our favorite), or serve with your favorite pasta dish.

 PREP TIME
15 minutes

 COOK TIME
6 to 8 hours

 SERVINGS
4 to 6

INGREDIENTS

- 1 lb ground turkey
- 1/4 cup plain bread crumbs
- 1/4 cup grated Parmesan cheese
- 1 egg
- 1 Tbsp Italian seasoning
- 1 (24 oz) jar marinara sauce

DIRECTIONS

1. Mix turkey, bread crumbs, Parmesan cheese, egg, and Italian seasoning in a medium bowl using your hands.
2. Divide mixture into 12 balls. You can eyeball this or use an ice cream scoop.
3. Pour sauce into a slow cooker. Carefully add meatballs.
4. Cover and cook on low for 6 to 8 hours or on high for 4 to 6 hours.

✳ PRO TIP

Okay, okay—I have another variation of this: Mix the ground turkey, bread crumbs, and egg. Roll the mixture into balls and place them in a greased baking dish. Bake at 400 degrees for 15 to 20 minutes. Remove the pan from the oven and top each meatball with a quartered slice of American cheese and return it to the oven until the cheese melts. Cheeseburger meatballs! If you're feeling fancy, skewer a piece of lettuce, a slice of tomato, and a sliced pickle on top.

Chicken Tortilla Soup

This was a staple in our house when the twins were babies. It's easy to make ahead and is one of our most beloved comfort foods. Serve a bowl with chips and salsa. Garnish with sour cream and avocado. Squeeze in the juice of a lime if you like your soup with a little kick. Dress up your chicken tortilla soup however you see fit!

PREP TIME
10 minutes

COOK TIME
6 to 8 hours

SERVINGS
6 to 8

INGREDIENTS

- 4 cups chicken broth
- 1 (15 oz) can black beans
- 1 (15 oz) can corn
- 2 (16 oz) jars red salsa
- 4 boneless skinless chicken breasts
- Optional: tortilla chips, salsa, sour cream, sliced avocado, lime wedges

DIRECTIONS

1. Drain and rinse beans and corn. In a slow cooker, combine broth, beans, corn, and salsa. (Yes, just dump them in and stir!)
2. Place chicken breasts on top. Add salt and pepper to taste.
3. Cover and cook on low for 6 to 8 hours or on high for 4 to 6 hours.
4. When chicken has reached an internal temperature of 165 degrees, remove the breasts to a plate and shred them with a fork. Return chicken to slow cooker.
5. Give it all another stir.
6. Serve with your favorite toppings.

Crunchy Ranch Chicken

Y'all aren't even ready for this recipe. It's going to become a home run, five-star hit in your house just like it is in ours. Pair this chicken with a veggie side and maybe some potatoes. Or use it to top your favorite salad.

 PREP TIME
10 minutes

 COOK TIME
25 minutes

 SERVINGS
4

delicious as a main dish or on top of a salad!

INGREDIENTS

- 1 1/2 cups cornflakes
- 1 (1 oz) packet ranch seasoning
- 1/2 cup grated Parmesan cheese
- 1/2 cup (1 stick) butter
- 4 boneless, skinless chicken breasts

DIRECTIONS

1. Preheat oven to 400 degrees. Line a baking sheet with parchment paper. If you have one, add a wire rack on top to allow chicken to crisp on the bottom.
2. Put cornflakes in a ziplock bag and crush them to small bits.
3. Add ranch seasoning and Parmesan cheese to the bag. Close bag and shake to mix.
4. In a small pan or in the microwave, melt butter and put it in a medium bowl.
5. Cover chicken with plastic wrap and pound it to about 1/4-inch thick using a meat mallet.
6. Dip each chicken breast first in melted butter, coating both sides, allowing any excess to drip off, then shake it in the bag with dry mix, fully coating each piece.
7. Lay chicken on wire rack atop baking sheet.
8. Bake for 20 to 25 minutes or until chicken has reached an internal temperature of 165 degrees.

✳ PRO TIP

If you don't have any cornflakes on hand, literally any crunchy food will do—pretzels, Goldfish crackers, crackers, or even bread crumbs. You can even skip the cornflakes and bake the chicken breasts coated first with melted butter then with ranch seasoning!

Slow Cooker Barbecue Ribs

I'll never forget my grandpa sitting in his chair at the end of the table, a paper napkin tucked securely into his button-down shirt, with a barbecued rib in hand. No one cleaned a rib bone quite like my grandpa. These ribs always bring that memory to life. They are tender, delicious, and so simple that you could make them on a weeknight or for a weekend barbecue. Serve with potato salad and fruit salad for a perfect meal.

PREP TIME
10 minutes

COOK TIME
6 to 8 hours

SERVINGS
4 to 6

INGREDIENTS

- 3 lb pork spareribs
- 1 yellow onion
- 1 (18 oz) bottle barbecue sauce

DIRECTIONS

1. Season all sides of ribs with salt and pepper, rubbing seasonings in for extra flavor.
2. Add ribs to the slow cooker.
3. Chop onion and add it on top.
4. Pour barbecue sauce over ribs and onions.
5. Cover and cook on low for 6 to 8 hours or on high for 4 to 6 hours.
6. Remove from the slow cooker and serve.

 PRO TIP

For a little extra crispiness, place slow-cooked ribs on a baking sheet and bake at 350 degrees for about 10 to 15 minutes.

Chicken Squares

I'm so grateful I've somehow ended up with friends who understand this season of life. We're all so busy. We love our families and love feeding them well. But we do not have four hours to spend in the kitchen each night. My friend Kristin Winchester sent me this recipe literally on this cookbook's manuscript due date. I had to squeeze it in because it is a winner!

PREP TIME
20 minutes

COOK TIME
15 to 17 minutes

SERVINGS
8

INGREDIENTS

- 4 chicken breasts, cooked and shredded
- 2 Tbsp mayonnaise
- 6 oz cream cheese, softened
- 2 cups shredded cheddar cheese
- 2 (8 oz) tubes crescent rolls

DIRECTIONS

1. Preheat oven to 350 degrees.
2. In a medium bowl, mix cooked chicken, mayonnaise, softened cream cheese, and shredded cheese together.
3. Unroll crescent roll dough and connect 2 dough triangles together to make 1 square. Repeat to make 4 squares.
4. Put one-quarter of chicken mixture into center of each square.
5. Fold dough over filling and pinch corners together to close in the center. Place them on a baking sheet.
6. Bake for 20 minutes.

Dinner
Assembly Meals

| assembly meal: | a quick, easy dish made by combining ready-to-use ingredients with little or no cooking. see also: lifesaver. |

Cheeseburger Salad

INGREDIENTS

- 1 lb ground beef
- 1 bag pre-chopped romaine lettuce
- 1/2 to 1 cup dill pickle slices
- 1 1/2 cups cherry tomatoes
- 1 cup shredded cheddar cheese
- 1/2 cup ranch dressing

DIRECTIONS

1. Brown ground beef over medium heat. Remove from heat and drain.
2. Divide lettuce evenly into salad bowls.
3. Add sliced pickles, halved tomatoes, and cheese to bowl. Stir.
4. Add ground beef.
5. Top with ranch or a dressing of your choice.

* PRO TIP

Ranch is a great dressing for this cheeseburger salad. But if you have extra time and ingredients on hand, try making this sauce, which is very similar to McDonald's Big Mac sauce: whisk together 1/2 cup mayonnaise, 2 Tbsp ketchup, 2 Tbsp dill relish, 2 tsp mustard, 2 tsp vinegar, 1/2 tsp paprika, and 1/2 tsp onion powder.

Cowboy Soup

INGREDIENTS

- 5 (15 oz) cans beans (different kinds)
- 1 (15 oz) can corn
- 1 (10 oz) can diced tomatoes with green chilies (we like Rotel)
- 1 (1 oz) taco seasoning packet
- 1 (1 oz) ranch seasoning packet
- 1/2 to 1 cup water

DIRECTIONS

1. Drain and rinse all beans. Add them to a large pot over medium-low heat.
2. Stir in corn, tomatoes with chilies, taco seasoning, and ranch seasoning.
3. Add 1/2 to 1 cup water, depending on your desired thickness, and stir.
4. Simmer uncovered for 15 minutes to 2 hours. The longer you simmer, the better the flavors will mix.

* PRO TIP

Approach cowboy soup like a chili. Serve with toppings such as shredded cheddar cheese, sour cream, avocado, jalapeño slices, cilantro, tortilla chips, and lime wedges.

Chicken Taco Salad

INGREDIENTS

- 4 boneless skinless chicken breasts
- 1 (16 oz) jar salsa
- Juice of 1 lime
- 1 (1 oz) packet taco seasoning
- 1 to 2 (11.5 oz) bagged salad kits

DIRECTIONS

1. In a slow cooker, combine chicken breasts, salsa, lime juice, and taco seasoning. Stir to coat chicken.
2. Cover and cook on low for 6 to 8 hours or on high for 4 to 6 hours.
3. Remove chicken and shred it with two forks. Return meat to pot and stir to combine.
4. Make bagged salad kit according to dircitons on the bag and top with the chicken.

Lazy Shepherd's Pie

INGREDIENTS

- 1 lb ground turkey
- 1 (12 oz) bag frozen mixed vegetables
- 1 (24 oz) package refrigerated mashed potatoes (we like Bob Evans)
- 1 cup shredded cheddar cheese

DIRECTIONS

1. Preheat oven to 350 degrees. Spray an 8 x 8-inch baking dish with nonstick cooking spray.
2. Brown ground turkey in a skillet over medium heat until it is cooked through. Season with salt and pepper (throw in a little garlic powder if you're feeling fancy).
3. Add frozen vegetables to pan and stir to thaw and warm.
4. Add turkey and veggie mix to baking dish.
5. Microwave mashed potatoes according to instructions on package. Spoon over turkey mixture. Top with cheese.
6. Bake for 15 to 20 minutes, until potatoes are lightly browned.

Clean-Out-the-Fridge Soup

INGREDIENTS

- 2 Tbsp olive oil
- 1 yellow onion
- 2 garlic cloves
- 4 to 6 cups of whatever veggies you have on hand (carrots, cabbage, broccoli, squash, zucchini, green beans, corn, peas, or kale)
- 4 cups vegetable broth
- 1 (28 oz) can crushed tomatoes
- Optional: shaved Parmesan cheese

DIRECTIONS

1. In a large soup pot or Dutch oven, add olive oil and warm over medium heat.
2. Chop onion and sauté for about 3 minutes, until translucent.
3. Mince garlic (or just use pre-minced garlic) and sauté 1 minute.
4. Chop and add hard vegetables such as carrots or broccoli. Stir and sauté for 5 minutes, or until the vegetables begin to soften, adding additional olive oil if needed.
5. Chop and add softer vegetables such as cabbage, squash, zucchini, green beans, corn, and peas. Sauté for 3 minutes, until they are warm.
6. Add greens such as kale, vegetable broth, and crushed tomatoes. Bring soup to a boil.
7. Cover and simmer 20 to 25 minutes.

Barbecue Pulled Pork

INGREDIENTS

- 1 yellow onion
- 3 lb pork tenderloin
- 1 (18 oz) bottle barbecue sauce (we like Sweet Baby Ray's)

DIRECTIONS

1. Spray your slow cooker with nonstick cooking spray (or add a liner).
2. Slice onion and place in bottom of slow cooker. Place pork tenderloin on top of onions.
3. Pour entire bottle of barbecue sauce over pork tenderloin.
4. Cover and cook on low for 6 to 8 hours or on high for 4 to 6 hours.
5. Shred pork with two forks, and mix with onions and sauce.
6. Serve with rolls for sandwiches or on its own with a side of veggies.

Baked Ravioli

INGREDIENTS

- 1 (24 oz) jar marinara sauce, divided
- 1 (20 to 24 oz) bag frozen ravioli
- 1 1/2 cups shredded mozzarella cheese
- 1 1/2 cups shredded Parmesan cheese

DIRECTIONS

1. Preheat oven to 375 degrees. Spray a 9 x 13-inch baking dish with nonstick cooking spray.
2. Pour about one-third of the marinara sauce into baking dish.
3. Top with half the ravioli, then half the mozzarella cheese.
4. Repeat layers, then top it with the Parmesan cheese.
5. Cover and bake for 30 minutes.
6. Uncover and bake for an additional 10 minutes.

Frito Pie

INGREDIENTS

- 2 (15 oz) cans chili*
- 2 (10 oz) cans diced tomatoes with green chilies (we like Rotel)
- 3 cups shredded Mexican-style cheese
- 6 snack-size bags of Fritos
- 1 bag pre-shredded romaine lettuce

DIRECTIONS

1. Preheat oven to 350 degrees. Spray a 9 x 13-inch baking dish with nonstick cooking spray.
2. Empty chili cans into a skillet over medium heat. Cook until warm.
3. In baking dish, layer half the chili, then 1 can of the tomatoes with chilies and half the cheese. Repeat layers.
4. Bake for 20 minutes or until cheese is bubbly.
5. Gently crush each bag of Fritos.
6. Spoon the chili mixture on top of the Fritos in individual bags.
7. Top with lettuce and serve with a fork for big smiles!

*Or sub 3 cups homemade chili

* PRO TIP
Serve with any toppings you like! A few ideas are sour cream, avocado, jalapeño slices, and cilantro.

BLT Sandwiches

INGREDIENTS

- 12 strips bacon
- 8 leaves lettuce
- 2 tomatoes
- 8 slices sourdough bread
- 4 Tbsp mayonnaise

DIRECTIONS

1. Preheat oven to 400 degrees. Loosely twist bacon (to fit more on the pan), and add to a baking sheet. Bake for 20 to 30 minutes.
2. While bacon cooks, wash and dry lettuce and tomatoes. Slice tomatoes and lettuce for sandwiches.
3. Toast the bread.
4. Spread the mayonnaise across one side of each slice of toast.
5. Assemble the sandwich: bread, bacon, tomato, lettuce, bread.

Shrimp & Grits

INGREDIENTS

- 2 cups milk
- 2 cups water
- 1 cup stone-ground grits
- 1/4 tsp salt
- 1 cup shredded cheddar cheese
- 4 Tbsp butter, divided
- 1 lb small shrimp, deveined and peeled
- 1 Tbsp Cajun seasoning

DIRECTIONS

1. In a medium pan, boil milk and water. Add grits and salt, then reduce heat. Cook until grits are soft, about 15 minutes. Stir in cheese and 3 Tbsp butter.
2. Warm remaining 1 Tbsp of butter in a skillet, and cook shrimp until they are no longer translucent, about 5 minutes. Top with seasoning like Slap Ya Mama (yes, it's really called that) or Tony Chachere's, but if you prefer your shrimp less spicy, you can simply use salt and pepper.
3. Top grits with the shrimp and enjoy!

Sheet Pan Parmesan Chicken & Broccoli

INGREDIENTS

- 1 (12 oz) bag frozen broccoli florets
- 1 Tbsp olive oil
- 4 boneless skinless chicken breasts
- 1/2 cup grated Parmesan cheese, divided
- 1/3 cup mayonnaise
- 1/2 cup bread crumbs, divided

DIRECTIONS

1. Preheat oven to 400 degrees.
2. Place broccoli on a baking sheet and drizzle with olive oil. Season with salt and pepper to taste.
3. Cover chicken breasts with plastic wrap and pound them out until they're roughly 3/4 inch thick. (It doesn't really matter how thick they are; you just want them all to be about the same thickness.)
4. In a bowl, mix most of the Parmesan cheese and all the mayonnaise, reserving a little cheese for topping.
5. Top each chicken breast with cheese mixture and then with breadcrumbs (save a little of these too).
6. Add chicken to baking sheet next to the broccoli.
7. Bake for 20 to 25 minutes or until the internal temperature of the chicken is 165 degrees.
8. A few minutes before everything is done, sprinkle the rest of the breadcrumbs and cheese on top of everything.

* PRO TIP
If you're feeling fancy, throw some quartered petite potatoes in with the broccoli at the beginning. Yum.

Mac & Peas

INGREDIENTS

- 2 (7.25 oz) boxes macaroni and cheese
- 1/2 cup milk
- 1/4 cup (1/2 stick) butter
- 1 cup frozen peas

DIRECTIONS

1. Make macaroni and cheese according to instructions on package.
2. Add frozen peas. Stir to warm and combine.

One-Pot Pasta Alfredo

INGREDIENTS

- 1 (16 oz) box fettucine pasta
- 1 (15 oz) jar alfredo sauce
- Whatever vegetable you have in the fridge or freezer (good options: broccoli, peas, or green beans)
- Whatever protein you have on hand, such as leftover chicken
- French bread, for serving

DIRECTIONS

1. Cook noodles according to the instructions on package, drain, and return to the pot.
2. Add jar of alfredo sauce. Continue to warm pasta on medium heat.
3. Chop vegetables into bite-size pieces, and add them to the pot and continue to cook.
4. Add any protein you may have on hand (or serve as a vegetarian dish).
5. Serve with warm French bread.

Sheet Pan Sausage & Veggies

INGREDIENTS

- 1 lb link sausage, sliced
- 3 bell peppers
- 1 yellow onion
- 1 lb baby potatoes
- 1 Tbsp olive oil
- 1 tsp dried oregano

DIRECTIONS

1. Preheat oven to 425 degrees. Line a baking sheet with parchment paper.
2. Slice sausage into 1/4-inch-thick pieces and add to the pan.
3. Slice peppers and onions into similar thicknesses, about 1/4 inch thick. Add them to the baking sheet. Quarter potatoes and add them to the baking sheet.
4. Drizzle with olive oil and season with oregano and salt and pepper to taste.
5. Bake for 25 minutes, then remove from the oven and toss. Smash potatoes with a fork, then bake for another 20 minutes.
6. Serve and enjoy!

Baked Ziti

INGREDIENTS

- 1 (16 oz) box ziti noodles
- 1 (24 oz) jar marinara sauce
- 2 cups shredded mozzarella cheese
- 1/2 cup grated Parmesan cheese
- French or sourdough bread from your local bakery, for serving (trust me on this one)

DIRECTIONS

1. Preheat oven to 350 degrees. Spray a 9 x 13-inch baking dish with nonstick cooking spray.
2. Cook noodles according to instructions on package.
3. Drain noodles, return them to the pot, and add marinara. Stir to warm and combine.
4. Dump mixture into baking dish. Top with mozzarella and then Parmesan cheese.
5. Bake for 10 to 15 minutes. You're just warming here, so if you're really hungry, let the cheese melt and take it out of the oven.
6. Serve with French or sourdough bread.

Sheet Pan Nachos

INGREDIENTS

- 1 lb ground beef
- 1 (15 oz) can black beans
- 1 (1 oz) packet taco seasoning
- 1 (13 oz) bag tortilla chips
- 2 to 3 cups shredded cheddar cheese
- 1 cup mild salsa
- Optional: sliced green onions, salsa, sour cream (or Greek yogurt), diced tomatoes, avocado, cilantro, lime

DIRECTIONS

1. Preheat oven to 350 degrees. Line a baking sheet with parchment paper.
2. Brown ground beef in a skillet over medium heat until it is cooked through. Drain the excess fat and discard.
3. Drain and rinse black beans, and add beans and taco seasoning to skillet, stirring to combine, and cook for an additional 3 minutes.
4. Line baking sheet with tortilla chips. Top with half the beef-and-bean mixture, then a layer of cheese. Repeat layers.
5. Bake for 5 minutes or until cheese is melted.
6. Remove the nachos from the oven and top with salsa and any other favorite toppings.

* PRO TIP

If you learn any kitchen hack from this book, let it be this: Spoon the sour cream (or Greek yogurt) into a baggie, and snip one of the bottom corners. Drizzle from the cut corner over your nachos. This will prevent giant clumps of sour cream on certain bites and none on others. You're welcome.

Open-Faced Sandwiches

INGREDIENTS

- 1 loaf fresh French bread
- 1/2 lb sliced deli ham
- 1/2 lb sliced provolone cheese
- 1/2 cup sliced green olives with pimentos
- Italian dressing, as needed

DIRECTIONS

1. Preheat oven to 350 degrees. Line a baking sheet with parchment paper.
2. Slice a loaf of French bread horizontally to make a top and bottom to your sandwich.
3. Place both sides face up on baking sheet.
4. Top one side with ham, then provolone cheese, then olives. Drizzle Italian dressing over sandwich.
5. Bake for 10 minutes or until cheese is melted. At the very end, turn broiler on (keep an eye on it, as food can burn quickly) to brown your bread and cheese ever so slightly.
6. Remove sandwich from the oven, slice, serve, and enjoy.

Barbecue Beef Sandwiches

INGREDIENTS

- 1 yellow onion
- 1/2 cup barbecue sauce
- 1 1/2 cups beef broth
- 3-lb chuck roast
- 1 (12-count) package Hawaiian sweet rolls

DIRECTIONS

1. Slice onion into long, thin pieces.
2. In a slow cooker, stir together barbecue sauce, beef broth, and sliced onion. Add chuck roast.
3. Cover and cook on low for 6 to 8 hours or on high for 4 to 6 hours.
4. Remove meat and shred it with two forks. Remove any fatty pieces.
5. Add shredded beef to Hawaiian rolls to make mini sandwiches, tapping off excess juice when removing beef from slow cooker to avoid soggy bread.

* PRO TIP

If you're feeling extra fancy, transfer the shredded beef to a baking dish and place it under the broiler in the oven (don't take your eye off it, as it can burn easily). Spoon the meat onto larger brioche roll bottoms, top each with a slice of provolone cheese, and melt that bad boy in the oven. Remove it from the oven, top with the other half of the bun, and go to town!

Loaded Broccoli

INGREDIENTS

- 1 (12 oz) steam-in-bag fresh broccoli florets
- 2 cups shredded cheddar cheese
- 5 strips bacon
- 1/2 cup sour cream, for topping

DIRECTIONS

1. Preheat oven to 350 degrees. Spray a 9 x 13-inch baking dish with nonstick cooking spray.
2. Steam broccoli according to the package directions.
3. Cook and crumble bacon.
4. Add broccoli to baking dish. Top with shredded cheese and bacon.
5. Bake for 5 minutes or until cheese is melted.
6. Top with sour cream (piping it from a baggie works best!) and serve.

French Dip Sandwiches

INGREDIENTS

- 2 to 3 lb chuck roast
- 1 1/2 cups beef broth
- 1 (2 oz) packet onion soup mix
- 1 loaf fresh French bread
- 1/4 cup (1/2 stick) butter
- 8 to 12 slices provolone cheese

DIRECTIONS

1. Add chuck roast to a slow cooker and top it with beef broth and onion soup mix.
2. Cover and cook on low for 6 to 8 hours or on high for 4 to 6 hours.
3. Shred meat with two forks, removing any fatty pieces.
4. Slice French bread in half horizontally and toast the halves, and then slice thickly.
5. Assemble sandwiches, placing a slice of provolone cheese on top of the meat in each one.
6. Serve with small bowls of "juice" (it's called *jus*, but we're just going to go with "juice" here) from the slow cooker for dipping.

Taco Bowls

INGREDIENTS

- 1 lb ground beef
- 1 (1 oz) packet taco seasoning
- 1 (15 oz) can black beans
- 1 (8 oz) bag steam-in-bag rice
- Shredded Monterey Jack cheese, for topping

DIRECTIONS

1. Brown ground beef in a skillet over medium heat. Drain excess fat and discard. Drain and rinse black beans. Add taco seasoning and black beans to pan. Mix well.
2. Heat bag of rice in microwave according to the instructions on package.
3. In bowls, layer rice, meat-and-bean mixture, and cheese, then any additional toppings.

* PRO TIP
Serve with any taco toppings you have on hand. We like to finish ours off with a squeeze of lime and either crushed tortilla chips or store-bought tortilla strips.

English Muffin Pizzas

INGREDIENTS

- 6 English muffins
- 1/2 cup pizza sauce
- 1 1/2 cups shredded mozzarella cheese
- 1/2 cup mini pepperoni
- Other pizza toppings, as desired

DIRECTIONS

1. Preheat oven to 375 degrees.
2. Split open English muffins and top each one with a spoonful of pizza sauce. Place them on a baking sheet.
3. Top with shredded cheese and pepperoni, then any other toppings you'd like.
4. Bake for 10 minutes.

* PRO TIP
For your toppings bar, set out caramelized onions, ricotta cheese, tomatoes, basil, cooked ground sausage, and pickled jalapeños.

Loaded Cheeseburger Fries

INGREDIENTS

- 1 (24 oz) bag frozen curly fries
- 1 lb ground beef
- 1 tomato
- 1 cup shredded cheddar cheese
- 1 bag pre-shredded lettuce

DIRECTIONS

1. Preheat oven according to the instructions on fries package.
2. Line a baking sheet with parchment paper, and dump fries onto sheet. Bake fries according to directions.
3. Brown ground beef in a skillet over medium heat until it is cooked through. Drain the excess fat and discard. Season with salt and pepper to taste.
4. Dice tomato and remove seeds—nobody wants mushy tomatoes on their fries. To do this, slice in half, then scoop out the seeds before dicing.
5. Top baked fries with ground beef then cheese, lettuce, and diced tomato.

Loaded Baked Potatoes

INGREDIENTS

- 4 russet potatoes
- 2 Tbsp olive oil or avocado oil
- 4 strips bacon
- 2 green onions
- 1/2 cup shredded cheddar cheese
- Sour cream, for topping

DIRECTIONS

1. Preheat oven to 400 degrees.
2. Rinse and pat dry potatoes, and poke them all over with a fork.
3. Rub potatoes with olive oil or avocado oil, and season with salt and pepper to taste.
4. Place on a baking sheet and bake for 1 hour, or until a knife pokes easily into the middle.
5. While potatoes are baking, fry bacon in a skillet until crispy, and chop it into bite-size pieces.
6. Slice green onions into 1/4-inch pieces.
7. Remove potatoes from the oven and make a small slit in the center of each one end to end. Squeeze from both sides to open them up to make space for toppings.
8. Top with cheese, bacon, sour cream, and green onions.

Chili Dogs

INGREDIENTS

- 4 hot dogs
- 4 hot dog buns
- 1 (15 oz) can chili
- 1/2 to 3/4 cup shredded cheddar cheese

DIRECTIONS

1. Cook hot dogs either by boiling them for 10 minutes, grilling them outdoors, or cooking them in a greased skillet for 10 minutes on medium.
2. Toast buns.
3. While hot dogs are cooking, empty chili into a small pan over medium heat, and warm it for 5 minutes.
4. Assemble and top with cheese, and then watch the smiles spread across your people's faces!

Chicken Quesadillas

INGREDIENTS

- Butter, for the pan
- 4 flour tortillas
- 1/2 cup shredded or chopped cooked chicken
- 3/4 cup shredded Monterey Jack cheese
- Optional: salsa, sour cream, and guacamole, to top

DIRECTIONS

1. In a skillet, melt a pat of butter.
2. Place one tortilla in the pan, then top it with half the chicken and half the cheese. Lay another tortilla on top.
3. Cook over medium heat until bottom of the tortilla starts to brown and cheese starts to melt. Flip and cook until it's toasty and melted. Repeat with remaining ingredients.

* PRO TIP
Serve your quesadillas with salsa, sour cream, and guacamole.

Sloppy Joes

INGREDIENTS

- 1 green bell pepper
- 1 lb ground beef
- 3/4 cup ketchup
- 1 (2 oz) packet onion soup mix
- 2 Tbsp brown sugar
- 4 hamburger buns

DIRECTIONS

1. Seed and finely dice bell pepper.
2. Brown ground beef and diced pepper in a skillet over medium heat. Drain the excess fat and discard.
3. Stir in ketchup, onion soup mix, and brown sugar. Continue to cook to combine flavors, about 5 minutes.
4. Spoon meat mixture onto buns and enjoy!

Charcuterie for Dinner

INGREDIENTS (OR ITEMS TO CONSIDER WHEN ASSEMBLING):

- Cheeses
- Crackers
- Nuts
- Bread or toast
- Deli meats
- Basically any leftovers (skewer with toothpicks for extra-fancy points)
- Pickles
- Hummus or dips
- Jams and spreads
- Bite-size veggies
- Bite-size fruits
- Olives

DIRECTIONS

1. Select a large tray for your charcuterie board. Grab a few small bowls for dips, spreads, and anything that may spill over the edge, like nuts.
2. Get out all the foods you can incorporate onto your tray.
3. Filling random spots as you go, line up crackers, add nuts to bowls, slice cheese blocks, and assemble your display.
4. Set your board in the center of the table and give everyone a small plate. Dig in!

Dessert

Dessert

Buckeyes

These bite-size peanut butter and chocolate desserts are great for serving a crowd or stashing in your fridge for midnight snacks. They're fun to make, so get the kids involved. Heads up: this recipe will need about an hour of cooling time.

PREP TIME
10 minutes

COOK TIME
Refrigerate 45 minutes to 1 hour total

SERVINGS
60 buckeyes

INGREDIENTS

- 1 1/2 cups smooth peanut butter
- 10 Tbsp butter, softened
- 1 tsp vanilla extract
- 4 cups powdered sugar
- 4 (4 oz) bars semisweet chocolate
- 2 tsp coconut oil

DIRECTIONS

1. Add peanut butter, softened butter, and vanilla to a mixing bowl. Mix with a hand mixer until it's light and fluffy.
2. Continue mixing while sifting in powdered sugar until it is firm and somewhat dry.
3. Roll the dough into 60 balls about an inch wide. Poke a toothpick into the top of each one. Place them on 2 parchment-lined baking sheets.
4. Freeze for 30 minutes or until chilled.
5. Chop chocolate bars and melt with coconut oil in a small saucepan over low heat.
6. Using toothpicks, dip the dough balls (buckeyes) into the melted chocolate, coating the bottom and sides but leaving part of the buckeye uncoated.
7. Place back on the lined baking sheet. Remove the toothpicks and refrigerate the buckeyes until the chocolate hardens.

Pound Cake

This recipe is so simple to make yet so impressive to serve. It's just delicious. Your whole family will argue over who gets to eat more of the crunchy part.

PREP TIME
10 minutes

COOK TIME
1 hour

SERVINGS
8

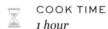
makes a great dessert... or breakfast

INGREDIENTS

- 1 cup (2 sticks) butter, softened
- 1 cup sugar
- 1 tsp vanilla
- 4 eggs
- 2 cups all-purpose flour
- 1/2 tsp baking powder
- 1/2 tsp salt

DIRECTIONS

1. Preheat oven to 350 degrees. Spray a loaf pan with nonstick cooking spray.
2. In a large bowl, cream butter and sugar with a mixer, about 4 minutes. Add vanilla, then eggs one at a time as you continue mixing.
3. Add flour, baking powder, and salt. Mix until thick and fluffy, about 3 minutes.
4. Pour cake batter into loaf pan, and bake for 1 hour or until toothpick inserted in the center comes out clean.
5. Let cool for 60 minutes before serving.

Pumpkin Pie

This has more than a few ingredients, but when it's all said and done, you'll be glad you made this version. This is my mother-in-law's recipe. Every Thanksgiving I make three pies: one for the family, one for Bryan, and one for Bryan's brother, Mike. The first pie is served traditionally with dinner, but the second two get eaten straight out of the pie plates.

 PREP TIME
10 minutes

 COOK TIME
3 hours
(refrigerate or
cool 2 hours)

 SERVINGS
8

INGREDIENTS

- 1 premade piecrust
- 1 1/2 cups canned pumpkin
- 2 eggs
- 1 1/2 cups evaporated milk
- 1/4 cup brown sugar
- 1/2 cup sugar
- 1/2 tsp salt
- 1 1/2 tsp ground cinnamon
- 1/2 tsp ground ginger
- 1/4 tsp ground cloves
- 1/4 tsp ground nutmeg
- 1/4 tsp ground allspice (my MIL's secret ingredient)

DIRECTIONS

1. Preheat oven to 425 degrees.
2. Unroll piecrust and place it in a 9-inch pie plate.
3. In a large bowl, whisk together pumpkin, eggs, and evaporated milk. Mix in rest of ingredients.
4. Pour mixture into piecrust.
5. Bake for 15 minutes. Then turn oven down to 350 degrees, and bake for another 40 minutes, until a knife inserted in the center comes out clean.
6. Remove pie from oven, let cool for 2 hours or refrigerate before serving.

 PRO TIP

My mother-in-law's pumpkin pie had a little something extra in it—a dash of allspice. She has since passed away, and now that's my secret ingredient and a way to keep her memory with us.

Peanut Butter Kiss Cookies

I could eat peanut butter straight from the jar. My dad and I used to enjoy a late-night snack of graham crackers and peanut butter while everyone else was asleep. My next favorite peanut butter dessert? These five-ingredient peanut butter cookies.

PREP TIME
10 minutes

COOK TIME
10 minutes

SERVINGS
12 cookies

INGREDIENTS

- 1 cup peanut butter
- 1/2 cup plus 2 Tbsp sugar, divided
- 1 egg
- 1/2 tsp salt
- 12 Hershey's Kisses

DIRECTIONS

1. Preheat oven to 350 degrees. Line a baking sheet with parchment paper.
2. Mix peanut butter, 1/2 cup of sugar, egg, and salt until well blended, then roll into 1-inch balls.
3. Roll balls in remaining 2 Tbsp of sugar. Place balls on baking sheet 1 inch apart.
4. Bake for 10 minutes. Remove pan from oven and press 1 unwrapped chocolate kiss into each cookie.
5. Allow cookies to cool for 10 minutes.

Simple Fudge Brownies

These brownies . . . don't bake them unless you want to be tempted to eat the whole pan!
They are fantastic and so very easy to make.

 PREP TIME
10 minutes

 COOK TIME
Varies
according to
brownie mix
instructions

 SERVINGS
12 brownies

my kids' favorite
dessert to make
on their own

INGREDIENTS

- 1 package brownie mix (we love Ghirardelli Double Chocolate)
- Milk (to replace water in brownie package instructions)
- Butter, melted (to replace oil in brownie package instructions)
- Eggs (as per brownie package instructions)
- 1/4 cup semisweet chocolate chips

DIRECTIONS

1. Preheat oven according to brownie package. Spray an 8 x 8-inch baking dish with nonstick cooking spray.
2. Following the brownie package instructions, combine brownie mix, milk, and melted butter in a medium bowl.
3. Stir in eggs.
4. Pour the batter into the baking dish, top with chocolate chips, and bake for time directed on brownie package.

✳ PRO TIP

Serve warm and top with vanilla ice cream. Yum!

Rainbow Dip

Do you remember those kid snacks—cookies with a dip that looked like Funfetti? You know the ones! Little animal crackers and that yummy, sweet dip, much like icing? Well, this is close enough to make you miss the snacks of the nineties!

PREP TIME
10 minutes

COOK TIME
*Refrigerate
1 hour*

SERVINGS
8

INGREDIENTS

- 1/2 (15.25 oz) box Funfetti cake mix
- 2 (8 oz) containers light Cool Whip
- 1 cup vanilla yogurt (not Greek)
- Rainbow sprinkles
- Teddy Grahams or animal crackers

DIRECTIONS

1. In a large bowl, mix cake mix, Cool Whip, and yogurt until well combined.
2. Cover the bowl with plastic wrap and refrigerate for 1 hour.
3. Remove the dip from the fridge, top with sprinkles, and serve with fun animal crackers.

Classic Chocolate Chip Cookies

Do you ever do something for your kids and it sort of fills up your mom tank? Baking my kids chocolate chip cookies does that for me. They're just so classic and make literally everyone happy. This recipe is simple, delicious, and easy to make.

 PREP TIME
10 minutes

 COOK TIME
10 to 12 minutes

 SERVINGS
24 cookies

INGREDIENTS

- 1 cup butter, softened
- 1 cup white sugar
- 1 cup brown sugar
- 2 eggs
- 1 tsp vanilla extract
- 1 tsp baking soda
- 1/2 tsp salt
- 3 cups all-purpose flour
- 2 cups semisweet chocolate chips

DIRECTIONS

1. Preheat oven to 350 degrees. Line 2 baking sheets with parchment paper.
2. In a large bowl, use a hand mixer to mix butter with white and brown sugars. Add egg and vanilla and continue mixing.
3. Add flour, baking soda, and salt and mix to combine, being careful not to overmix. Stir in chocolate chips.
4. Place spoonfuls of dough on baking sheets 1 inch apart.
5. Bake for about 10 to 12 minutes.
6. Remove cookies from oven and allow to cool for 2 minutes.

 PRO TIP

Ever heard of Monster Cookies? These were Brady's favorite when he was itty bitty. Basically, when mixing in the chocolate chips, add any other small treat you like (nuts, M&M's, Reese's Pieces, and so on).

Banana Pudding

Sadly (and oddly), I'm allergic to bananas. But the rest of the people in my house absolutely love banana pudding. This is an easy recipe for a gathering or to pleasantly surprise your people after supper.

 PREP TIME
*10 minutes
(refrigerate 1
hour)*

 COOK TIME
0 minutes

SERVINGS
8 to 12

INGREDIENTS

- 1 (3.4 oz) box vanilla *or* banana pudding mix
- 2 cups milk, for the pudding
- 1 (11 oz) box vanilla wafers
- 5 bananas, sliced
- 1 (8 oz) container Cool Whip, thawed

DIRECTIONS

1. Prepare pudding according to instructions on package.
2. Arrange half the vanilla wafers on the bottom of a 9 x 13-inch baking dish.
3. Using the back of a big spoon, spread half the pudding over the vanilla wafers. Top with a single layer of banana slices. Repeat layers, reserving some banana slices for topping.
4. Spread Cool Whip over the top layer of bananas and top with a few more bananas.
5. Refrigerate at least 1 hour.

Rice Krispies Treats

These no-bake bars take me back to being six years old. I got to help dump the Rice Krispies into the bowl *and* lick the spoon. This classic recipe will make even the grown-ups smile. Heads up: this recipe will need at least an hour of cooling time.

PREP TIME
10 minutes

COOK TIME
*5 minutes
(refrigerate
1 hour)*

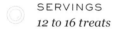

SERVINGS
12 to 16 treats

INGREDIENTS

- 3 Tbsp butter
- 1 (10 oz) package miniature marshmallows
- 6 cups Rice Krispies cereal

DIRECTIONS

1. Spray a 9 x 13-inch baking dish with nonstick cooking spray.
2. In a large pan over medium-low heat, melt butter.
3. Add marshmallows and stir mixture until marshmallows are fully melted, then remove pan from heat.
4. Add Rice Krispies and stir until well coated.
5. Spoon mixture into baking dish, and use a spatula to spread it evenly. Refrigerate for 1 hour.

Chocolate Truffles

There is nothing I love more than a flourless chocolate cake. Straight chocolate goodness—no crust, no raspberries, no nuts—just chocolate heaven. I digress. Flourless chocolate cake takes a little more work than I'm usually willing to put in, so these truffles are the next best thing. Heads up: this recipe requires at least one hour of extra time for the truffles to cool in the fridge. Also, if you'd prefer this to be dairy-free, sub full-fat coconut milk for the heavy cream (same amount).

 PREP TIME
10 minutes

 COOK TIME
Refrigerate 90 to 120 minutes total

 SERVINGS
24 truffles

INGREDIENTS

- 2 (4 oz) chocolate bars (60% to 75% cacao)
- 1/2 cup heavy cream
- 1/2 cup cocoa
- Optional: sprinkles, finely chopped nuts, or coconut, for topping

DIRECTIONS

1. Finely chop chocolate bars and add pieces to a medium bowl. Pour in heavy cream and microwave for about 1 minute. Whisk until smooth.
2. Refrigerate for 30 to 60 minutes, until mixture is firm enough to scoop.
3. Remove chocolate mix from the fridge and use an very small ice cream scoop or a cookie dough scoop (it should hold about 1 Tbsp of dough) to scoop out about 24 balls. (Alternatively, pour mixture into an 8 x 8-inch baking dish before refrigerating, leave the chocolate in the dish, and simply slice it into squares and top it with cocoa.)
4. Roll chocolate balls with your hands. (Warning: this can get sticky. Coat your hands in cocoa, make sure they're very cold, or wear gloves to avoid messy hands. If the chocolate is still too sticky, pop it back in the fridge for a few more minutes.)
5. Place toppings in bowls and roll each ball in the topping of your choice.
6. Refrigerate the balls again for 60 minutes. Remove them from the fridge at least 15 minutes before serving.

Dessert
Assembly Meals

| assembly meal: | a quick, easy dish made by combining ready-to-use ingredients with little or no cooking. see also: lifesaver. |

Chocolate Mousse

INGREDIENTS

- 1 (3.9 oz) package instant chocolate pudding
- 1 1/2 cups milk, for the pudding
- 1 (8 oz) container original Cool Whip, thawed
- Optional: additional container of Cool Whip for topping

DIRECTIONS

1. Whisk together chocolate pudding mix and milk. Fold in the Cool Whip.
2. Refrigerate mousse until ready to serve, at least 1 hour.
3. To serve, spoon mousse into cups or bowls, then top with more Cool Whip, if using.

Simple Whipped Cream

INGREDIENTS

- 2 cups heavy whipping cream
- 3 to 4 Tbsp powdered sugar
- 1 tsp vanilla extract

DIRECTIONS

1. About 30 minutes before you make the whipped cream, put your mixing bowl and the beaters from your mixer in the fridge. This is a really important step.
2. Add whipping cream to chilled bowl, and mix until soft peaks form. Add powdered sugar and vanilla, and continue mixing until it holds medium-stiff peaks.
3. Once you see peaks, stop! Don't overmix, or you will make butter. Serve same day.

Frozen Banana Treats

INGREDIENTS

- 3 bananas
- 1 (12 oz) bag semisweet chocolate chips
- 2 tsp coconut oil

DIRECTIONS

1. Line a baking sheet with parchment paper.
2. Slice bananas about 1/2 inch thick and set aside.
3. Add chocolate chips and coconut oil to a medium microwave-safe bowl. Stirring in between 30-second intervals, microwave mixture until chocolate is fully melted.
4. Using a fork, dip bananas into chocolate and place them on the baking sheet.
5. Freeze bananas for 2 hours.

Cookie Skillet

INGREDIENTS

- 1 (30 oz) roll refrigerated cookie dough
- Vanilla ice cream

a crowd favorite!

DIRECTIONS

1. Preheat oven to 375 degrees.
2. Press cookie dough into a 10-inch cast-iron skillet, covering the entire bottom of the skillet.
3. Bake for 15 minutes, until edges are golden and center has set.
4. Allow cookie to cool for 10 minutes, then slice into wedges and top with a few scoops of ice cream.

Pretzel Bites

INGREDIENTS

- 1 (16 oz) bag small pretzels
- 1 (10.6 oz) bag Rolo candy
- 1 (10 oz) bag M&M's

DIRECTIONS

1. Preheat oven to 200 degrees. Line a baking sheet with parchment paper.
2. Line up pretzels on the sheet, covering the whole area. Place 1 Rolo on top of each pretzel.
3. Place baking sheet in oven, keeping an eye on it, and remove the sheet when chocolate begins to look shiny.
4. Top each Rolo with 1 M&M, and allow candy and pretzels to cool completely.

Strawberry Shortcake

INGREDIENTS

- 1 (16 oz) container fresh strawberries
- 1/4 cup sugar
- 1 (12-count) package shortcake dessert cups
- 1 (6.5 oz) can whipped topping

DIRECTIONS

1. Slice strawberries and place them in a medium bowl. Toss them with the sugar, and refrigerate until sugar dissolves.
2. Spoon strawberries into dessert cups, and top with whipped topping.

* PRO TIP
There are so many ways to customize this recipe. You can swap the shortcakes for biscuits, mash your strawberries a little for more texture, or make homemade whipped cream.

Monkey Bread

INGREDIENTS

- 3 (16.3 oz) cans refrigerated biscuits
- 1 cup sugar
- 2 tsp cinnamon
- 1/2 cup (1 stick) butter
- 1 cup brown sugar

DIRECTIONS

1. Preheat oven to 350 degrees. Spray a Bundt pan with nonstick cooking spray.
2. Using kitchen scissors, cut biscuits into quarters.
3. Mix sugar and cinnamon in a gallon-size ziplock bag.
4. Working in batches, add biscuit pieces to bag and shake to coat them with cinnamon-sugar. Place coated biscuit pieces in Bundt pan.
5. In a small saucepan over medium-high heat, melt butter and brown sugar, boiling for 1 minute.
6. Pour sauce over biscuits.
7. Bake for 35 minutes.
8. Let cool for 10 minutes, then flip Bundt pan over to slide out monkey bread.

Ice Cream Cookie Sandwiches

INGREDIENTS

- 1 dozen store-bought bakery cookies
- 1 quart ice cream
- 1/2 cup rainbow sprinkles
- 3/4 to 1 cup Magic Shell chocolate-flavored topping

DIRECTIONS

1. First, put your cookies in the freezer for at least 30 minutes so they don't break during sandwich building.
2. While the cookies are getting colder and firmer, take the ice cream out of the freezer for about 10 to 15 minutes to soften. You don't want it to be melted, but you do want it to be pliable. Pour the sprinkles onto a plate and pour the Magic Shell into a bowl.
3. When you're ready, scoop one scoop of ice cream onto the bottom of one cookie. Top with another cookie, the bottom side facing the ice cream, so both cookies are top out, and press the cookies together until the ice cream spreads to the edges.
4. Roll the ice cream sandwich across the plate of sprinkles. Dip half the ice cream sandwich into the Magic Shell.

Chocolate Fondue

INGREDIENTS

- 2 (12 oz) bags milk chocolate chips
- 1 cup heavy cream
- Bananas, strawberries, pound cake, donut holes, marshmallows, or Rice Krispies Treats, as needed, cut into bite-size dippers

DIRECTIONS

1. Combine chocolate chips and heavy cream in a microwave-safe bowl and microwave for 1 minute. Stir. Microwave again in 30-second intervals until chocolate is fully melted.
2. Transfer chocolate-and-cream mixture to a heavy medium-size bowl or fondue pot. If it starts to thicken too much while you're eating, simply microwave it another 30 seconds or add a little bit more heavy cream to thin it.
3. Skewer your favorite dippers, dip them into the chocolate, and enjoy!

Baked Apples

INGREDIENTS

- 4 red baking apples
- 2 Tbsp butter
- 1/4 cup brown sugar
- 1 tsp cinnamon

DIRECTIONS

1. Preheat oven to 350 degrees. Spray a 9 x 13-inch baking dish with nonstick cooking spray.
2. Peel and chop apples into bite-size pieces. Place in the baking dish.
3. In a small saucepan, melt butter, then stir in brown sugar and cinnamon. Pour mixture over apples and toss to coat.
4. Bake for 20 minutes.

Sheet Pan S'mores

INGREDIENTS

- 24 graham crackers
- 1 (12 oz) bag large marshmallows
- 6 large chocolate squares
- 6 regular Reese's Peanut Butter Cups

DIRECTIONS

1. Place your oven rack on the lowest rack possible. Preheat the broiler.
2. Line a baking sheet with 12 graham cracker squares.
3. Top each graham cracker with either a chocolate square or a Reese's Peanut Butter Cup. Place 1 marshmallow on top of each.
4. Place baking sheet in the oven, and watch it for 1 to 3 minutes to ensure marshmallows don't burn.
5. Remove baking sheet when marshmallows are golden brown and puffed up.
6. Top immediately with the remaining graham cracker squares.

* PRO TIP

Get creative with your chocolate! There are so many fun chocolate flavors to choose from—mint, raspberry, caramel. Have fun!

Cream Cheese Fruit Dip

INGREDIENTS

- 1 (8 oz) block cream cheese, softened
- 1 (7 oz) jar marshmallow creme
- Strawberries, pineapple, cantaloupe, grapes, or blueberries, cut into bite-size pieces, for dipping

DIRECTIONS

1. Place cream cheese and marshmallow creme in a medium mixing bowl. Blend with a hand mixer until smooth.
2. Place cream mixture in a serving bowl, and serve with your favorite fruits.

SECTION FIVE

Fancy

ell

These recipes are for when you're feeling a little more fancy.

My Mom's Lasagna

I don't know that my mom ever intended for this recipe to become "the family recipe," but it sure has! We all love it! She adapted her version from my grandmother's, and together, we adapted her version into a simplified version. I'm excited to share it with you here. It's a go-to meal for celebration dinners, birthday gatherings, and Sunday suppers with friends. For the marinara, we like Rao's Homemade. Note: you will not use all the noodles in the box for this recipe.

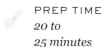

PREP TIME
20 to
25 minutes

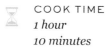

COOK TIME
1 hour
10 minutes

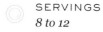

SERVINGS
8 to 12

a family favorite for special occasions

INGREDIENTS

- 1 lb ground sausage
- 1 lb ground chuck
- 4 Tbsp Italian seasoning, divided
- 2 (24 oz) jars marinara sauce
- 2 eggs
- 1 (16 oz) container cottage cheese (we like Good Culture)
- 1 cup grated Parmesan cheese
- 2 tsp garlic powder
- 1 (10 oz) box no-bake lasagna noodles
- 2 cups shredded mozzarella cheese, divided

DIRECTIONS

1. Preheat oven to 350 degrees. Spray a 9 x 13-inch baking dish with nonstick cooking spray.
2. In a large skillet or Dutch oven, brown sausage and ground chuck over medium heat. Drain the excess fat and discard.
3. Add 2 Tbsp of Italian seasoning and both jars of marinara sauce to the meat.
4. Simmer meat mixture uncovered while you do the next steps, stirring occasionally.
5. Whisk eggs in a mixing bowl. Add cottage cheese, Parmesan cheese, garlic powder, and remaining 2 Tbsp of Italian seasoning to the eggs.
6. In the 9 x 13-inch baking dish, add a scoop of meat sauce (this will keep noodles from sticking). Then layer half the noodles, half the cheese mixture, half the mozzarella, and half the meat sauce.
7. Repeat layers. If you have any extra cheese, throw some on top.
8. Bake uncovered for 45 minutes.
9. Let the lasagna cool for 15 minutes before serving. This step is super important!

Jambalaya

Maybe it's because we live on the Gulf of Mexico, or maybe it's because one of my favorite meals ever is our friend Mike's jambalaya (he's New Orleans born and raised), but I had to include a simplified version of this delicious Cajun dish. Remember, the meat thermometer is your friend: 165 degrees internal temperature = done.

PREP TIME
25 minutes

COOK TIME
35 minutes

SERVINGS
6 to 8

INGREDIENTS

- 2 boneless skinless chicken breasts
- 6 oz andouille sausage
- 1 yellow onion
- 2 green bell peppers
- 2 Tbsp olive oil
- 1 garlic clove
- 1 tsp dried oregano
- 2 cups chicken broth
- 1 (15 oz) can crushed tomatoes
- 1 cup uncooked white rice
- 2 tsp Old Bay seasoning
- 1 lb medium shrimp, peeled and deveined

DIRECTIONS

1. Cut chicken into 1-inch pieces and sausage into 1/4-inch pieces.
2. Dice onion and deseed and dice peppers. Mince garlic.
3. Heat olive oil in a large pot over medium heat. Add chicken and sausage and cook until done, about 5 minutes.
4. Add onion and peppers to pan. Sauté until onions are translucent, about 5 minutes. Add garlic and oregano, and sauté 1 minute more.
5. Add chicken broth, crushed tomatoes, rice, and Old Bay seasoning.
6. Stir and cover, cooking until rice has absorbed the liquid, about 20 minutes. Be sure to stir occasionally to avoid it sticking.
7. Add shrimp and cook until they are pink, about 5 minutes.
8. Remove from heat and let the jambalaya sit for 5 minutes. Fluff it with a fork, and let it rest 5 minutes more before serving.

Cast-Iron Filet Mignon

Our family loves a good ol' steak dinner, so I'm excited to include a steak recipe here. They often make steaks on the grill, but during the colder months, it's nice to know how to make them indoors. The cast-iron skillet used in this recipe helps give this filet a great char.

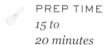

PREP TIME
15 to
20 minutes

COOK TIME
15 minutes

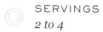

SERVINGS
2 to 4

INGREDIENTS

- 2 to 4 (6 oz) filet mignon steaks
- 1/2 cup (1 stick) salted butter, softened
- 2 Tbsp fresh rosemary
- 2 Tbsp fresh parsley
- 2 Tbsp fresh chives
- 1 garlic clove
- 2 Tbsp olive oil
- Mashed potatoes, for serving

DIRECTIONS

1. Remove steaks from the fridge 30 minutes before cooking.
2. Chop fresh herbs. In a small bowl, mix softened butter, rosemary, parsley, chives, and garlic. Set bowl in the fridge.
3. Preheat oven to 425 degrees.
4. Pat steaks dry with a paper towel. Season both sides with salt and pepper to taste.
5. Heat a cast-iron skillet over medium-high heat until it is just barely smoking.
6. Add some olive oil, then the steaks.
7. Sear steaks on each side for 3 minutes and 1 additional minute around sides.
8. Using an oven mitt (the handle and pan will be hot), move skillet to oven.
9. Bake steaks for about 4 minutes, or until the desired temperature is reached. The steaks will continue cooking

Continued. . .

for about 5 minutes once removed from the oven, so keep that in mind. The final temperatures in the center of each steak should be:

- Rare: 125 degrees, cool red center
- Medium rare: 130–135 degrees, warm red center
- Medium: 140–145 degrees, warm pink center
- Medium well: 150–155 degrees
- Well: 160+ degrees

10. Remove skillet from the oven. Transfer steaks to a plate to rest for 5 to 10 minutes.
11. Top each steak with a pat of herb butter and serve with mashed potatoes.

Cooking Temps

Knowing cooking temperatures is crucial for ensuring food safety and proper cooking. Below are a few guidelines recommended by the USDA (United States Department of Agriculture) and the FDA (Food and Drug Administration).

Refrigerator temperature to keep foods safe	40 degrees
Temperature to keep cooked foods hot	135 degrees
Safe internal temperature for whole cuts of meat and seafood	145 degrees
Safe internal temperature for ground meats	160 degrees
Safe internal temperature for poultry and leftovers	165 degrees
Common oven temperatures for baking	300 to 350 degrees
Common oven temperatures for roasting	375 to 400 degrees

Use a food thermometer. One of the most reliable ways to ensure that food is cooked safely and to the correct temperature is by using a food thermometer. Insert the thermometer into the thickest part of the food, away from bone or fat, to get an accurate reading of the internal temperature. This is especially important for meat, fish, and leftovers.

Follow recommended guidelines. Different types of foods require different cooking temperatures to ensure that they are safe to eat. It's essential to follow recommended guidelines for cooking temperatures to prevent foodborne illnesses by ensuring that harmful bacteria are destroyed during cooking.

Let food rest. After removing food from heat, let it rest for a few minutes before serving or slicing. This resting period allows the internal temperature of the food to stabilize and allows the juices to redistribute throughout the meat. Keep in mind that food continues to "carry-over cook" even after it's been removed from the heat. To prevent overcooking, especially with meats, it's important to remove them from the heat source when they're slightly below the desired internal temperature. This allows for carryover cooking to bring the food up to the safe temperature while preventing it from becoming overcooked and dry.

Substitutions

Oops! I'm out of _____! No worries! You can more than likely substitute something you do have on hand for something you don't. Below are twenty common substitutions to keep in mind when you forget something at the grocery store.

OUT OF THIS?	USE THIS INSTEAD.
Baking powder	1/4 tsp baking soda + 1/2 tsp cream of tartar
Baking soda	Use 2 to 3x the amount of baking powder
Brown sugar (firmly packed)	1 cup granulated sugar + 1 Tbsp molasses
Butter (for baking)	margarine, vegetable shortening, or coconut oil (equal amount)
Butter (for sautéing)	olive oil, vegetable oil, or ghee
Buttermilk	1 cup milk + 1 Tbsp lemon juice or vinegar
Buttermilk (for pancakes or waffles)	1 cup plain yogurt or sour cream + a little milk
Eggs (for binding)	1 Tbsp ground flax seeds or chia seeds + 3 Tbsp water
Eggs (for leavening, baking)	1/4 cup applesauce or mashed bananas
Half-and-half	1/2 cup whole milk + 1/2 cup heavy cream
Heavy cream	3/4 cup milk + 1/4 cup melted butter
Powdered sugar	Blend 1 cup sugar + 1 Tbsp cornstarch until fine
Rice vinegar	White wine vinegar OR cider vinegar (equal amount)
Sour cream	1 cup plain yogurt + 1 Tbsp lemon juice or vinegar
Soy sauce	Mix equal parts Worcestershire sauce + water
Tomato sauce	Blend 1 cup canned tomatoes or tomato paste with water
White wine vinegar	Lemon juice or apple cider vinegar (equal amount)
Whole milk	1/2 cup evaporated milk + 1/2 cup water

Index

Acknowledgments

I have genuinely never been part of a more collaborative book. First and foremost, thank you to my longtime literary agent, Claudia. This book was a dream for many years. Your guidance and wholehearted belief in what it could and would become helped get it over the finish line in more ways than one. Thank you for endlessly believing in this book and in me.

MacKenzie, Sabryna, Marilyn, Kristen, Kristi, Sara, and Emily (and everyone I am forgetting to add). I appreciate, more than anything, your willingness to let my intuition lead the way with this special book. Choosing to write a book about the topic that has challenged me the most in my life as a busy woman was . . . an adventure. But I knew that, together, we could create something so useful and helpful. Thank you for envisioning magic where there once was none.

Jen Gott—book eleven. We did it! Thank you for every red line, every encouraging text, and every way you make my writing better.

Brittany, Whitney, Carly, Laura, Dusty, Taylor, Liz, Lindsey—more affectionately known as Team Simplified. Your names each belong on the cover of this book. Thank you for lending your incredible individual talents to every word, every recipe, every photo, every page, and every graphic in here. I'm equally grateful for your abilities to be the best hype squad there ever was. For a book that took about six hundred years to write, it needed the best cheerleaders—or at least its author did. Thank you. I've had the time of my life fighting dragons with you.

Jane, Jen, and Lea—my Pensacola besties. You are my village. My people when I'm up against a deadline (again) and I have two kids who need rides and one kid who forgot their lunch box. I never dreamed I'd have sisters one day, but here we are.

Mom, Dad, Brett, and Taylor—mi familia. The trophy you gave me for cooking the best Thanksgiving turkey ever that one year is still one of my most prized possessions. And while I don't quite loathe being in the kitchen anymore, I'm still staking my claim on "table decorating" on the list of Thanksgiving responsibilities. Mom and Dad, thank you for telling me I could be anything I ever wanted, even if it was quite literally crazy. Join the circus? "We'll be in the front row." Write a cookbook? "Wait . . . you? Well, okay! We'll be first in line for a signed copy!" I love you all with all of me.

Bryan—we did it. We got this labor of love over the finish line. You believed in me when I didn't believe in myself, just like you always do. Thanks for holding down the fort while I wrote and tested endless recipes. Thanks for trying bites of all of it, even the fails. And thanks for pushing me, since day one, to topple over the obstacles when racing toward the impossible. You're my person, and I love you.

Brady, Tyler, and Caroline. Mom wrote a cookbook. HA! I know, right?! Let this be a forever reminder that you—*yes, you!*—can do literally anything. Never count yourself out. Don't let any doubt hold you back. Your quirks and "weaknesses" might just be your superpowers. Thank you for cheering me on during this entire journey. I love each of you with every fiber of me. Being your mom is the greatest joy of my whole life.

About the Author

Emily Ley is the founder of Simplified®, a bestselling brand of planners and organizational tools for busy women found online and in Target, Walmart, Office Depot, and Staples.

She has spent more than sixteen years empowering, inspiring, and equipping women in the areas of organization, planning, and simplicity. She is the author of eleven books and a best-selling Substack. Emily has been featured in *Forbes*, *Glamour*, and *Good Housekeeping* and was recognized as Entrepreneur of the Year by Studer Community Institute. She also serves on the Board of Advisors for the Rally Foundation for Childhood Cancer Research and was recently inducted into the University of West Florida College of Business Hall of Fame.

Now, as an author, entrepreneur, wife, and mother to three, Emily lives in Pensacola, Florida, with her husband, Bryan, their son Brady, and twins Tyler and Caroline. She enjoys flourless chocolate cake, organizing junk drawers, and trading dog memes with her teenager.

Let's be friends!

- @emilyley
- @simplified
- emilyley.com
- emilyleybooks.com
- emilyley.substack.com